THE AUTHOR

RAY C. HACKMAN is Research Director of
the Psychological Service of Pittsburgh.
He received his A.B. and M.A. in psychology at the University of Nebraska and his
Ph.D. at the University of Minnesota.

the
MOTIVATED
WORKING ADULT

the
MOTIVATED
WORKING ADULT

Ray C. Hackman

American Management Association, Inc.

Foreword

THE FIELD OF PERSONNEL PSYCHOLOGY has developed tools for measuring the abilities and aptitudes that predict a person's capacity to carry out a wide variety of work tasks. Measures of interests and values are useful in career counseling and to some extent in industrial selection. However, until now neither measures of work motivation nor, indeed, any agreement on a theory of work motivation or its precise definition existed. This book reports a series of research efforts that have made significant contributions to both the theory of work motivation and its measurement.

The study of the motivation of men and women at work has been the broad concern of Psychological Service of Pittsburgh (PSP) and its research program since 1954. This study program has been carried on in several stages under two research directors. The first phase of the program, directed by Frederick Herzberg, reviewed the literature on job attitudes.[1] The second phase, also directed by Dr. Herzberg, was an adaptation of the critical incident technique used to obtain information on high and low periods of job satisfaction and is reported in *The Motivation to Work.*[2]

After Dr. Herzberg left PSP to assume a teaching and research post at Western Reserve University, Ray Hackman became research director at PSP and continued with the studies of work motivation. This book reports the research done under his direction.

Financial support for the research program has come from a variety of sources. Initially it was provided by the Buhl Foundation on condition that matching funds be obtained from private industry. Industrial support, at first, came through specific grants to research in which PSP was then engaged. More recently, industrial companies have contributed to the research effort—and continue to contribute—by annual membership fees as PSP associates. The list of companies that follows includes both types of industrial contributors.

[1]F. Herzberg *et al., Job Attitudes: Review of Research and Opinion,* Psychological Service of Pittsburgh, 1957.
[2]F. Herzberg *et al., The Motivation to Work,* John Wiley & Sons, Inc., New York, 1959.

The Alcoa Foundation

Allegheny Ludlum Steel Corporation

Bacharach Industrial Instrument Company

Bell Telephone Company

Bessemer & Lake Erie Railroad

Blaw - Knox/Company

The Buhl Foundation

Butler County Mushroom Farm, Inc.

Columbia Steel and Shafting Company

Copperweld Steel Company

Crucible Steel Company of America

Dravo Corporation

Duquesne Light Company

Edgewater Steel Company

Femco, Inc.

Fidelity Trust Company

General Nutrition Corporation

Gulf Oil Corporation

Harbison - Walker Refractories Company

W. S. Hill Company

Homestead Valve Manufacturing Company

Horix Manufacturing Company

Jones & Laughlin Steel Corporation

Kay Richards & Company

Latrobe Steel Corporation

Levinson Steel Company

Marbon Chemical Division of Borg - Warner Corporation

McCreary Tire and Rubber Company

McKinney Manufacturing Company

Mellon National Bank & Trust Company

Mesta Machine Company

Mine Safety Appliances Company

The Office of Naval Research

Peoples First National Bank & Trust Company

Pittsburgh National Bank

Pittsburgh Plate Glass Company

H. H. Robertson Company

Rockwell - Standard Corporation

The Rust Engineering Company

St. Joseph Lead Company

Scaife Company

Sealtest Foods

Spang & Company

Superior Steel Corporation

United States Steel Corporation

Universal - Cyclops Steel Corporation

West Penn Power Company

Westinghouse Electric Corporation

Williams & Company, Inc.

Both the board of directors and the staff of PSP appreciate the support that has come from the industrial community, from foundations, and from the Office of Naval Research. The kind of research described here can be carried on only by an organization with access to data on many different populations of people at work. Future stages of the research program will broaden our understanding of work motivation and its role in the lives of men and women not only in industry but also in other facets of our complex modern society.

Dora F. Capwell, Director
Psychological Service of Pittsburgh

Preface

MUCH OF THE EARLY WORK reported in this book was supported by a contract between the Office of Naval Research and the Psychological Service of Pittsburgh. Denzil D. Smith, at that time director of the Psychological Sciences Division of the Office of Naval Research, was instrumental in arranging for this support, and I should like to express my appreciation for his efforts.

For PSP and myself, I should like to acknowledge a debt to Otis C. McCreery, Arthur M. Doty, and the Alcoa Foundation for a grant made specifically to finance the writing of this book.

PSP itself contributed to the financial support of the research effort, and the financial and moral support of the board of directors and of individual members thereof is gratefully acknowledged.

Since 1958 a number of men and women have made noteworthy contributions to the collection, analysis, and interpretation of the material presented here. I should like to express my appreciation for their efforts more fully but must be content with just naming them: Dale Brown, Evelyn Hrapchak, Lynn Matherne, Thomas Mayor, Ruth Reichman, and George Todd.

Two of my professional colleagues made sizable contributions both to the development of the ideas on work motivation theory and to its exposition. They are Dale W. Dysinger in the earlier phases of the work and William L. Radtke in the later phases. To William Radtke I owe a special debt for writing and editorial help. The manuscript has also profited from critical reviews by A. W. Ayers, Roy B. Hackman, and Alan M. Kershner. However, I must assume responsibility for any errors of omission or commission still in the manuscript.

Dora F. Capwell, director of PSP, has been a continuing source of support and inspiration. Without her active encouragement the program of research reported here might have phased out long ago. Similar support has characterized the professional staff of PSP.

I have been blessed with a succession of research secretaries whose dedication to this program has gone considerably beyond the call of duty. In chronological order they are Susan Cornell, Peggy Stewart Butcher, Francine Smith, and Eileen Walsh.

Finally, may I express my deepest appreciation to my wife, Frances, and to our children, Robert and Carolyn, who shared with me the frustrations and rewards accompanying the research and its communication.

RAY C. HACKMAN

Pittsburgh, Pennsylvania

Contents

Exhibits

I

Introduction

THIS BOOK IS AN INTERIM REPORT of the research findings on one phase of the overall program that has been in progress at the Psychological Service of Pittsburgh (PSP) since 1958. Although the program is continuing and no date has been set for its conclusion, 1967 marked the completion of a significant phase in efforts to define and measure the work motivation characteristics of employed men and women. This is primarily a report of the research phase and is only peripherally concerned with theoretical issues.

Much of the research that has been done on the problem of motivation in humans, and probably to an even greater extent in animals, has concentrated on its role in learning. Because much of the theory in the field of motivation is an integral part of, or is ancillary to, learning theory, this basic interest in learning has occasioned the use of animals and students as experimental subjects.

Many years ago I became interested in motivation as one aspect of the problem of performance; that is, the differential exercise of a person's social, intellectual, perceptual, and motor skills. However, I was unable to describe and, hence, to measure motivation in adult men and women. It was therefore difficult to talk meaningfully about the development of such a characteristic or to definitively research the impact of incentive or reinforcement systems on performance. Even though motivation in adults could not be described accurately, it was assumed that individual differences in motivation were extensive, and the impact of particular incentives on groups of people would be difficult to assess.

Research on adult work motivation has taken a somewhat different tack. The Hawthorne Studies[1] on the behavior of factory workers set the stage here, and only in the past decade has attention been seriously directed toward the motivation of salaried workers at higher occupational levels. Research has pursued a number of directions: Some of it examines the conditions that surround an individual at work, seeking to identify and evaluate those that produce changes in his performance and, by implication, affect his motivation. Others examine the effects of very specific influences — for example, incentive systems, wage increases, and the like — on performance. Still others distinguish between well-motivated and poorly motivated workers or describe the characteristics of "motivating" environments.

A critical survey of the substantial and increasing literature on adult work motivation is beyond our present purposes. An excellent summary may be found in Saul W. Gellerman's *Motivation and Productivity*[2] and a shorter review in G. V. Barrett's *Motivation in Industry.*[3] The outcomes of these research efforts still are largely restricted in scope and do not provide principles of work motivation that apply generally across different groups and work conditions. Furthermore, the results of systematic research have not played a major role in shaping prevailing concepts of work motivation. Such influence has been wielded by works that are more "ideological" than empirical and that periodically occupy the bestseller list — for example, W. H. Whyte, Jr.'s *The Organization Man*[4] and Vance Packard's *The Status-Seekers.*[5] Such books advance answers to questions about what people work for, especially what motivates them in that most vital sector of our economy — industry. The books are rarely, if ever, based on systematic investigation or controlled research, but

[1] F. J. Roethlisberger and W. J. Dickson, *Management and the Worker,* Harvard University, Cambridge, 1933.

[2] American Management Association, New York, 1963.

[3] Howard Allen, Cleveland, 1966.

[4] Simon and Schuster, New York, 1966.

[5] David McKay, New York, 1959.

are most often written—and very well written—from the vantage of an informed observer. What emerges is a cohesive view that is typically *unidimensional* in the sense that it advances one motive—status, money, approval, or whatever—as the driving force of people in industry and treats other motives as organized about or instrumental to this one.

A similar tendency is evident in research efforts to explore a single motive. For example, D. C. McClelland's work on the achievement motive has advanced rapidly from the status of an empirical effort concerned with definition and measurement[6] to that of an ideological enterprise.[7] The effect of focusing on a single motive is naturally to centralize it in the cognitive field, with other motives organized in a secondary or dependent relation with respect to it. One thus arrives at a perspective on the world of work that may be quite cohesive and intelligible, but the question remains open whether this perspective is actually shared by men and women in industry; that is, whether they are in fact motivated in this fashion.

The results of the research reported here suggest that the single-motive approach is misleading. It will soon be seen that this research is distinguished by its nonideological origins. At no time was the role of informed observer assumed. People in industry described work experiences of particular significance to them, and the role of PSP was to try to discover some order in their accounts. These pages spell out in detail the steps in the investigation and what was found. With respect to prevailing concepts, however, the findings clearly indicate that a *multidimensional* concept is necessary to comprehend the work motivation of men and women. No single motive or motivational pattern is central to, or sufficient to account for, the work of men and women in modern industry.

This is not surprising. American industry has been developing and expanding as a vital social institution for more than a century. On the face of it, it indeed would be surprising if the division and specialization of function and the complex social ramifications of this development did not accommodate, and even call for, a corresponding variety of motivational characteristics. In fact, any attempt to characterize the men and women fulfilling the multitude of roles in this complicated social structure in terms of a single motive or motivational pattern must be regarded as, at best, outmoded and, at worst, an abortive venture in stereotyping.

[6]D. C. McClelland *et al., The Achievement Motive,* Appleton-Century-Crofts, New York, 1953.

[7]*The Achieving Society,* D. Van Nostrand, New York, 1961.

One need not go far in this book to find traces of many of the motives that form the singular themes of many prevailing conceptions. Thus achievement (McClelland), status (Packard), money and wealth (W. F. Whyte and Heilbroner), and approval (Crowne and Marlowe) are all represented here. The presence of these motives suggests that such conceptions are founded on an element of truth—an important factor in their persuasiveness. Two additional factors are required, however, to account for communication as effective as that represented by some of these books: the influence of (1) motivational set itself and (2) social attitude.

What appears to be significant to a person is a reflection of his own intentions and motivations. Likewise, what impresses a person as a convincing explanation of the behavior of others is influenced by what appears to him to be significant. Thus a writer interpreting the world of work will tend to construe it in the light of his own motivational set and, if he is an effective writer, will communicate with particular appeal to those similarly motivated. Moreover, a writer is influenced by current social attitudes that condition the kinds of motives he is inclined to attribute, or is willing to see attributed, to others. Industry has long been heir to ideological sentiments of one kind or another. Unfortunately, those who write and talk about the work motivations of people in industry are rarely themselves in industry and, thus, may be characterized by quite disparate kinds of motivation. The fact that their work is different from the work done by people in industry may account for their habitual tendency to deny that work itself is intrinsically satisfying in the industrial context. Our results clearly do not support this denial, and it seems time that this bias was laid to rest along with that of the monolithic character of industrial work motivation.

These two subjective influences point to the conclusion that prevailing concepts of work motivation in industry are subject to a good deal of projection that plays a selective role in what appeals to a person as a convincing explanation of work motivation. On this basis, we might feel that the multidimensional conception derived from our data has no great prospect of appealing to anyone. (On the other hand, it may have appeal simply because there is a little something in it for everyone.)

Much of the evidence presented here is based on information obtained by asking people to describe themselves. Some of it was gathered in questionnaires that asked for descriptions of what happened to these people at work and how they felt as a consequence. Some of it was obtained from a self-descriptive inventory of the temperament or personality test type.

Personality test inventories have a peculiar significance in the light of recent developments in this country. Within the past few years a number of people in the United States have made concerted attacks on the personality test as an invasion of privacy. Its use in the government has been banned by the Civil Service Commission, except in the selection of certain critical personnel. Although the particular temperament inventory used in this research was not an object of direct attack in the Congress, it has been tarred with the same brush. The objections are of two types: First, to ask people about their innermost thoughts and feelings is an invasion of privacy and is not to be tolerated; second, no one has been able to demonstrate the validity of these inventories in the selection of people for particular jobs.

Regarding the first objection, refusal to respond to these questions as well as to any other set is obviously a man's personal right. However, if he has a right to refuse, he also has a right to respond to them if he sees fit, and this right should not be abrogated by the Civil Service Commission or any other agency of government.

At PSP we have found very few individuals unwilling to respond to questions of this or any other appropriate type. People expect to answer questions about themselves, just as they expect answers to their questions about the jobs they are considering. The usual adult working in industry does not interpret questioning as a threat, but he does reserve the right to refuse to answer questions that appear to him to be inappropriate, and he exercises that right.

Regarding the second objection — that there is no direct evidence of the validity of these instruments in the selection of people for specific jobs — the evidence presented in this book speaks for itself. Answers to questions of the type used here do have predictive validity when interpreted against a background of specific statistical evidence.

Some psychologists also attack the use of personality and temperament tests, but for two somewhat different reasons. Their main criticism lies in the assumption that people are either incapable of honestly answering questions about themselves or unwilling to do so. The charge, which is based on evidence gleaned primarily from college students, is that people answer these questions in a socially approved fashion, rather than in terms of their own personal experience. There is no doubt that people can answer these questions in the light of what is approved in their own subculture, but evidence presented in this research strongly suggests that ordinarily they do not bother to do so. The second objection raised by psychologists is that answers to such questions are inherently so unreliable as to make them unusable for either routine statistical description or the development of theory. Until the time the statistical analyses reported here were performed this statement seemed valid, but it seems valid no longer.

The organization of the material in the following chapters is based on a chronology that describes the way in which the research program developed. The first chapter in the sequence (Chapter 2) describes a re-analysis and reinterpretation of Herzberg's[8] data that was performed in 1958 and was incorporated in an Office of Naval Research report appearing in 1961.[9] Chapter 3 describes the formal use of motivation items in a companywide attitude survey and subsequent statistical analyses performed on the data. The purpose of this step in the program, completed in 1962, was to broaden the base of the ideas contained in Herzberg's data by using a different method of data collection and broadening the sampling to include men at all levels in the industrial hierarchy. The third phase, reported in Chapters 3 and 4, encompassed the development of a structured questionnaire to measure the motivational characteristics of adult workers and the administration of this questionnaire to approximately 800 men, mostly salaried employees, seen routinely for psychological appraisal. This stage, initiated in 1963, was completed in January 1965.

From 1965 through 1966, these questionnaires were scored for the motivation factors found in the Herzberg and survey data. Men scoring high and low on these factors were contrasted by examining their responses to the items in a self-descriptive inventory. This resulted in the development of homogeneous subsets of items, the responses to which further described work-motivated men. This phase was completed in the summer of 1966 and is reported in Chapter 4. Chapter 5 describes the statistical properties of scales built from these item subsets and presents data on the way working men and women in a variety of jobs describe themselves on the scales. Chapter 6 is concerned with demonstrating, by means of factor analysis methods, the extent to which patterns of motivational characteristics are invariant across widely divergent groups of employed men and women. Chapter 7 presents evidence on the predictive validity of these ways of describing motivation in adults. Chapter 8 summarizes the preceding chapters by indicating the implications of the data

[8] F. Herzberg et al., The Motivation to Work, John Wiley, New York, 1959.
[9] R. C. Hackman and D. W. Dysinger, A Theory of Motivation, Technical Report, The Office of Naval Research, Pittsburgh, Contract Nonr-2810(00), June 1961.

for work-motivation theory. Chapter 9 discusses the practical implications of the data and theory in the selection, management, and development of people at work.

In the main, these data are technical, in the sense that their interpretation requires some statistical sophistication. Highly technical material has been placed in the six appendixes at the end of the book for the convenience of those interested in statistical procedures. Chapters 8 and 9 are deliberately written for readers more interested in the outcomes of the research than in the operations that produced those outcomes.

Finally, this book attempts to describe as accurately as possible how this research program developed. Much of it was designed as new insights were gained into the problem. It is to be hoped that future research on work motivation will profit not only from the designs that were effective but also from those that were not.

2

A Second Look
at Herzberg's Data

IN THE 1950'S a research team headed by Frederick Herzberg, then research director of Psychological Service of Pittsburgh, undertook an empirical study of the job attitudes of a group of 200 engineers and accountants. This study was completed in 1959 and the results were published under the title of *The Motivation to Work*.[1]

The method used in studying job attitudes consisted of a semistructured interview in which the men were asked about episodes in their work histories when they were very happy or very unhappy with their jobs. These episodes were critical in the sense that they represented periods of extraordinary affect. They were not all incidents, however, since they could last for long as well as for short periods of time.

Once an episode was identified by a respondent, he was asked to describe the condition or event that produced the feeling of happiness or

[1]John Wiley, New York, 1959.

20

unhappiness. Then he was asked to interpret the situation or event; that is, to talk about what it meant to him or how he felt about it at the time. Finally, he was asked to describe what effect, if any, the experience had on his job performance, attitudes, and mental health. This procedure was repeated for as many episodes as the man was willing to discuss.

Each kind of question elicited a specific kind of information. The first described events and conditions on the job that were satisfying or dissatisfying to the individual. The second described feeling states that apparently bore some relationship to states such as hunger and fear but were obviously a different class of experiences. The third described long- or short-range effects of the experience.

The interview protocols were analyzed for content, and coding schemes were developed for summarizing the information contained in the protocols. The analysis reported here is based solely on the first two kinds of data: job conditions and feelings. Before undertaking the analysis, a few minor changes were made in Herzberg's nomenclature and assignment of subcategories to make the major categories more meaningful. Thus Exhibits 1 and 2 differ somewhat from similar data reported by Herzberg.

THE PLEASANT OR SATISFYING EPISODES

Few conditions and events were named as having caused feelings of happiness; these tended to be self-oriented or task-oriented. The feeling states accompanying happy episodes appeared to have little specific emotional significance and were reported as having a pleasant feeling tone. A relatively simple statistical tabulation (Exhibit 3) showed that the eight feeling states reported in conjunction with the happy episodes could be differentiated into two subsets on the basis of their frequency of mention in association with specific events and conditions. This differentiation suggested that men identifying specific experiences accompanying generally pleasant feeling states were furnishing information about their motivation and about effective reinforcers in the job situation. These men were deriving satisfaction from two supplementary but divergent kinds of experiences: those intrinsic to the stimulation received from the specific tasks they performed as accountants or engineers and those intrinsic to the stimulation received from relating and interacting with people. Feelings of material and financial progress and of security also were reported by these men, suggesting the existence of extrinsic reinforcers.

A more detailed analysis of the interviews and the results follows.

Job Conditions

Exhibit 1 shows the percentage of men who reported specific job conditions as "causes" of their good feelings. Six conditions were mentioned with some frequency by these men. Four represent distinct changes in

EXHIBIT 1

Percentage of Men Reporting Specific Events or Conditions on the Job as "Causes" of Happy Episodes

	Long Range $N=80$	Short Range $N=96$
Events		
*1. Successful completion of a task	48	38
*2. Praise	20	49
*3. Increase in rank	9	24
*4. Increase in pay	11	19
Conditions		
*5. Work itself	51	4
*6. Supervisory responsibility	41	9
7. Permissive supervision	14	2
8. Status	10	7
9. Subordinates	9	3
10. Friendly supervision	5	4
11. Growth potential	6	3
12. Peers	9	0
13. Competent supervision	6	0
14. Personnel policies	2	3
15. Organization of work	2	3
16. Working conditions	3	0
17. Job security	2	0

*Only these frequently occurring events and conditions were selected for use in subsequent analyses.

the conditions surrounding a man on the job. The other two, being types of job activity, are continuously present.

By *work itself* these men meant the everyday activities on the job requiring the exercise of individual intellectual, perceptual, and motor skills. Supervision is also a job activity, but one requiring the exercise of specialized interpersonal skills. These men reported, then, that work is rewarding in its own right.

Successful completion of a task, praise, increase in rank, and *increase in pay* were the most frequently occurring events reported by these men and presumably the most important specific sources of satisfaction a job had to offer them. These four events are special cases of a familiar set of incentives to learning (knowledge of results, praise, and reward), which have been extensively researched by psychologists.

Feelings

The second type of data is uniquely an expression of feeling. The men interviewed used words like "accomplishment," "responsibility," "growth," and the like, or words and expressions similar in meaning, in describing how they felt. The terms used in Exhibit 2 are, in part, interpretations. The specific words "accomplishment," "recognition," "growth," "responsibility," "confidence," and "security" occurred in the protocols together with other phrases having equivalent meanings. The feeling of status was inferred from descriptions of feeling states — that is, feelings of "being somebody" — that suggested status to the coders of this material. The word "status" rarely appeared in these protocols.

Feelings of wealth were inferred from descriptions of economic gain or economic growth. The ideas expressed suggested that "the acquisition of material wealth or goods" was the significant interpretation attached to a particular event or condition. A promotion might give rise to feelings of recognition or status in one man, but might be interpreted by another as more money or evidence of financial progress.

Analysis and Interpretation

As with Herzberg's analyses, the total set of episodes was arranged into four subsets: one consisting of long-range happy episodes; a second

EXHIBIT 2

Percentage of Men Reporting Specific "Feelings" During "Happy" Episodes

Feelings	Long Range N = 80	Short Range N = 96
*1. Recognition	45	70
*2. Accomplishment	63	51
*3. Personal growth	43	43
*4. Responsibility	48	20
*5. Confidence	28	34
*6. Status	25	19
*7. Wealth	11	20
*8. Security	10	9
9. Belonging	14	9
10. Pride	8	7
11. Fairness	0	3

*Only these eight "feelings" were used in subsequent analyses.

consisting of short-range happy episodes; a third consisting of long-range unhappy episodes; and a fourth consisting of short-range unhappy episodes. The number of episodes in each subset was reduced so that no man was represented more than once in each grouping.

The analysis of job conditions was straightforward and is reported as Exhibit 1. We simply counted the number of men reporting each condition in connection with experiencing either happy or unhappy or long or short episodes, thus providing insight into their importance as sources of job satisfaction.

The feelings were a different matter. Exhibit 3 shows the percentage of men who reported each of the job conditions in association with each of the feelings. These data are based only on the long-range elated or happy episodes. The entries in this exhibit show the percentages of men who reported the indicated feeling as following or accompanying the specific job condition. For example, of the 50 men who reported a feeling of accomplishment accompanying satisfaction, 70 percent cited successful completion of a task as a main cause of that satisfaction; 44 percent listed supervisory responsibility as a primary cause of the satisfaction. Only 6 of the 16 job conditions in the original code occurred with sufficient absolute frequency to be used in this kind of analysis.

EXHIBIT 3

**Percentage of Men Reporting Specific Events and
Conditions on the Job
Concurrently with Specific "Feelings"***

Job Factors				*Feelings*				
	Recog- nition	Confi- dence	Accom- plish- ment	Status	Respon- sibility	Growth	Wealth	Secu- rity
1. Task completion	42	50	70	39	36	30	44	38
2. Praise	36	32	26	17	16	9	11	38
3. Increase in rank	15	9	4	17	13	15	44	0
4. Increase in pay	20	0	8	11	10	18	33	13
5. Work itself	50	50	60	56	49	42	33	63
6. Supervisory responsibility	48	45	44	73	62	50	33	25
Percent reporting the feeling	45	28	63	25	48	43	11	10

*Long-range "happy" episodes ($N = 80$).

In Exhibit 3 the feeling words have been ordered to bring out a start-ling relationship to job factors. Not only do the first three — recognition, confidence, and accomplishment — appear with sizable frequency in re-sponse to successful completion of a task, supervisory responsibility, work itself, and praise, but in addition the sets of relative frequencies exhibit a systematic increase or decrease. For example, the relative frequency of mention of successful completion of a task increases from recognition to confidence to accomplishment.

The second set of three feelings also shows a hierarchical arrangement, but the relative frequency of mention of specific job conditions is different in this set and in the first one. For example, both successful completion of a task and supervisory responsibility decrease in frequency of mention from status to responsibility to growth.

Exhibit 4 is particularly rewarding for those interested in replicated information. It presents the corresponding data for the short-range elated episodes. This exhibit should be interpreted in the same manner as Exhib-it 3. It shows even more strikingly the two clusters of feelings and, even more dramatically, illustrates the presence of the same two hierarchi-cal arrangements.

EXHIBIT 4

Percentage of Men Reporting Specific Events and
Conditions on the Job
Concurrently with Specific "Feelings"*

Job Factors			Feelings					
	Recog-nition	Confi-dence	Accom-plish-ment	Status	Respon-sibility	Growth	Wealth	Secu-rity
1. Task completion	29	45	62	6	11	14	5	22
2. Praise	51	57	54	28	27	24	21	66
3. Increase in rank	20	12	16	56	42	38	53	11
4. Increase in pay	20	12	10	22	21	17	53	33
5. Work itself	0	0	4	17	5	5	5	0
6. Supervisory respon-sibility	9	6	4	6	11	19	0	0
Percent reporting the feeling	70	34	51	19	20	43	20	9

*Short-range "happy" episodes ($N = 96$).

Significance of the Data

These data began to make sense when we formulated four hypotheses about motivation for work.

Hypothesis 1. The positive feelings produced by specific reinforcing events and conditions in the work situation signify the presence of *motivational states.* Since these feelings occur after, rather than before, the reinforcing event, the reinforcing agent must be presumed to maintain or augment the motivational state rather than to reduce it.

Hypothesis 2. Two fundamental *motivation channels* are suggested by the patterning of these feeling words. The first channel is reinforced primarily by the successful completion of a task. The second channel is reinforced primarily by being given supervisory responsibility.

Hypothesis 3. The extent to which a man's perceptual, motor, intellectual, and social skills have developed can be inferred from the specific verbal labels he uses to describe his reactions to reinforcing agents.

Consider the triad of recognition, confidence, and accomplishment. The events and conditions primarily instrumental in producing these feelings are work itself, successful completion of a task, and praise. Work itself generates satisfying experiences and, hence, is rewarding in its own right. Successful completion of a task represents closure in a sequence of activities that the individual perceives without additional supporting evidence.

Men reporting a feeling of *recognition* may be experiencing closure but may need supporting evidence (praise) from others. Men reporting feelings of *confidence* have become partially emancipated from reliance on others to support their perception of their accomplishment. Men reporting feelings of *accomplishment* need no support for their perception of the "goodness" of their performance.

These feelings can be interpreted as signifying the presence of *accomplishment* motivation, and men with this type of motivation can be called *closure seekers.*

The feeling triad of status, responsibility, and growth is produced by a somewhat different set of agents: supervisory responsibility, work itself, a promotion, and the successful completion of a task. The critical agent here is supervisory responsibility. A reasonable hypothesis is that these feelings occur in response to activities involving social interaction. The first two feelings, status and responsibility, reflect a man's positive interaction with the members of the groups with which he is identified. The third feeling, growth, implies emancipation from group identification.

Hypothesis 4. A third type of reinforcement appearing in these data seems to be extrinsic to work. Money is a symbol for a variety of things that can produce satisfaction. A feeling of security appears to be produced by events not integrally tied to the work a man is doing. Money may be an end in itself. It may be a device that shortens the time required to reduce physiological tensions. It may represent a means by which one can reduce or eliminate emotional tension by permitting escape from or attack on objects that are threatening or irritating. It may mean status. It may serve the same function as does praise. Security, of course, has at least four connotations. Basically it refers to what one *has* — money, acceptance, prestige, or specific motor, social, or intellectual skills.

THE UNPLEASANT OR DISSATISFYING EPISODES

Many more conditions and events were named by the interview respondents as causing feelings of unhappiness than were named as causing feelings of happiness. These conditions and events tended to be other-people- or situation-oriented in the case of the unhappy episodes. The feeling states accompanying these episodes tended to have specific emotional significance and an unpleasant affective tone. A pattern of associations existed among clusters of feeling states that accompanied pleasant episodes; no such pattern occurred among those accompanying unhappy episodes.

Data collected in the Herzberg study relative to periods when men were unhappy on their jobs differed markedly from those relative to the periods when they were happy. None of the job factors mentioned with reference to the pleasant or satisfying episodes occurred with any sizable frequency, except work itself. Supervision, personnel practices, and to a lesser extent the organization of work were assigned significance by these men in describing conditions that existed when they were unhappy on the job. The three most frequently reported feelings were "injustice," "shame or personal inadequacy," and "blocks to growth." No meaningful pattern emerged when these negative feelings were examined in relation to job conditions. Reports of unhappy episodes yielded one kind of information; reports of happy episodes yielded another kind. These men said that their work environment and the work they were doing did not stimulate them and contained many frustrations that produced unpleasant feeling states.

One set of data gives insight into things that reinforce motivation for work; the other set yields information on things likely to interfere with it. The former set describes the positive aspect of work motivation and the latter describes the negative aspect.

A REINTERPRETATION

This interpretation differs somewhat from the two-factor theory of Herzberg's. It agrees with Herzberg that things producing satisfaction on the job are qualitatively different from those producing dissatisfaction. It differs in the interpretation placed on a person's feelings in response to conditions and events in the job situation that generate satisfaction or dissatisfaction.

The feelings reported in association with unpleasant episodes signify states of emotional tension, are unpleasant in tone, and generally describe frustration, aggression, or anxiety reactions. The fact that any one job condition can generate a variety of emotional responses suggests individual differences in the tendency to be generally threatened or irritated by work rather than to respond to the specific frustrations of a job. Men responding in this fashion to their work may be described as emotional in temperamental makeup rather than as hygiene seekers. These people are not seekers; they are responders.

Herzberg describes men who derive satisfaction from their work as *motivation seekers.* The bulk of modern neurophysiological evidence on the functioning of the human central nervous system suggests that they could be described more appropriately as *stimulation seekers* and that their stimulation comes from either (1) the exercise of particular perceptual, motor, and problem-solving skills or (2) interaction with other people. Money furnishes an intermediate device through which extra-work stimulation of either type can be obtained.

It is reasonable to assume that the emotional tension produced in a man by his work environment is mediated by a different neurophysiological system, is essentially disruptive in character, and interferes with the stimulation-seeking activity.

As far as motivating people on the job is concerned, the basic problem appears to be one of discovering how to channel a man's energy in the direction of useful work. The clues to solving this problem may very well be contained in the data collected by Herzberg. Succeeding chapters describe attempts to further identify and refine these ideas about the nature of work motivation and the characteristics of motivated adults.

3

A Device for Measuring
Motivation for Work

THE THEORY OF ADULT MOTIVATION described in Chapter 2
suggests certain hypotheses regarding the motivation of employed adults.
Some of these are readily testable; others require research designs that
cannot be implemented in a short space of time.

Many people have objected to the methodology used by Herzberg
in his original study. Serious doubt has been expressed as to whether
one can generalize about information on 200 engineers and accountants —
although in *Work and the Nature of Man*[1] Herzberg summarizes subsequent research done by others on additional samples of employed men
and women. The type of interview used in the original study is generally
considered unreliable, and competent researchers question the validity
of data based upon reports regarding events even in the recent past.

[1]World Publishing Co., New York, 1966.

USE OF THE MOTIVATION ITEMS IN ATTITUDE SURVEYS

In order to introduce a greater degree of objectivity into the interrogation process and at the same time test the general applicability of the interpretation presented in the preceding chapter, a second phase of the research program was begun. A questionnaire variant of the structured interview was developed in the following fashion: The categories of events or conditions mentioned by the original respondents as causes of good feelings on the job were assembled in a list that a person could check as having been of significance in a given recalled episode. A similar list containing the feeling categories was also assembled. These two sets were presented with directions asking the person to think about a time he got a real "kick" out of his job and then to check the events or conditions and the feelings that applied at the time.

Similarly, a second pair of lists was constructed, one containing events and conditions reflecting potential sources of dissatisfaction, the other itemizing the unpleasant feelings accompanying them. The instructions to think of a time that the interviewee was made unhappy on the job and the pair of lists were designed to get at dissatisfaction on the job. The second pair of lists included the negative aspect of many of the items on the first pair of lists and encompassed others not appearing in the first pair. This questionnaire was incorporated as one section of an attitude survey administered for other purposes to all employees of a medium-size chemical firm. In this way, data were collected on reinforcers and feelings in an operational setting from many occupational levels.

The men and women in the company identified themselves in terms of broad administrative groupings and in terms of whether they were salaried or paid on an hourly basis. A number of separate subgroups in the company could be differentiated according to the jobs these people did and the job level at which they operated. These subgroups included:

1. Salaried outside salesmen.
2. Salaried supervisors and managers.
3. Salaried quality control industrial engineers.
4. Hourly production workers.
5. Hourly maintenance workers.
6. Salaried project and plant engineers.
7. Salaried development engineers and technicians.
8. Salaried research chemists and technicians.

Exhibit 5 illustrates both the similarities and differences in the motivation systems of men belonging to these occupational groupings, showing the percentage of men in each group who checked each of the conditions or events as producing happy states. The column on the right of the exhibit summarizes the relative frequency of mention of the several job conditions based on the 459 people represented in all of these subsamples.

EXHIBIT 5

Percentage of Men in Selected Job Groups Identifying
Particular Events and Conditions on the Job
as Sources of Satisfaction from Work

Sources of Satisfaction	Occupational Groups*								
	I	II	III	IV	V	VI	VII	VIII	Total
Interesting work	86	64	76	75	84	68	75	67	74
Successful completion of a task	79	54	55	53	68	83	66	51	56
Praise	64	43	66	47	48	40	52	53	49
Raise	29	36	34	37	30	29	34	33	34
Promotion	14	34	11	7	15	4	15	9	13
Permissive supervision	67	36	45	31	51	43	42	51	41
Work of subordinates	0	57	16	13	19	25	12	13	19
Supervision of others	0	45	32	16	22	18	16	24	21
Increased status	21	20	16	10	11	0	8	9	11

*I: 14 outside salesmen; II: 44 production supervisors and managers; III: 41 quality control industrial engineers; IV: 135 hourly production workers; V: 79 hourly maintenance workers; VI: 28 engineers; VII: 73 development engineers and technicians; VIII: 45 research chemists and technicians. Total = 459.

It is apparent from this that events and conditions that reinforce task-oriented motivation are of primary significance to these men and that this type of motivation is characteristic of men at all levels. Only in the line production groups is there any sizable percentage of men who report events or conditions reinforcing people-oriented or situation-oriented motivation, and these men are in managerial and supervisory jobs. Staff functions tend to be handled by individuals with task-oriented motives who derive their satisfaction most frequently from closure experiences. It is also significant that a raise as a reinforcing agent is mentioned with about the same frequency by all of these groups. Note that the two hourly groups responded to these items in much the same way as did the several salaried groups.

Exhibit 6 shows the percentage of men in each occupational group who reported each of the feeling experiences. A comparison of Exhibit 5 with Exhibit 6 indicates that these men reported more feeling experiences than reinforcers, suggesting that a single reinforcing agent produces a pattern of feeling responses. From Exhibit 6 it is apparent that these men reported the reinforcement of task-oriented motives most frequently. Only in the case of the managerial-supervisory group did many men report feeling states — responsibility and growth — tied to situation-oriented reinforcers. The rank ordering of these feelings can be obtained from the right-hand column of Exhibit 6 and again reflects the greater frequency of mention of task-oriented motives.

EXHIBIT 6

Percentage of Men in Selected Job Groups Identifying Particular Feelings Accompanying Satisfying Experiences on the Job

	Occupational Groups[*]								
Feelings	I	II	III	IV	V	VI	VII	VIII	Total
Accomplishment	93	82	76	68	74	75	77	80	74
Confidence	79	73	74	83	81	82	81	84	80
Pride	79	70	68	59	59	64	59	62	62
Recognition	86	68	76	53	73	50	66	67	62
Security	57	41	63	59	40	39	41	56	49
Acceptance	50	43	50	64	50	46	38	36	49
Financial progress	79	41	42	56	44	39	34	53	47
Importance	57	25	21	28	24	14	26	31	26
Growth	64	70	61	47	47	57	56	60	54
Responsibility	57	66	39	28	32	43	26	33	35

[*]I: 14 outside salesmen; II: 44 production supervisors and managers; III: 41 quality control industrial engineers; IV: 135 hourly production workers; V: 79 hourly maintenance workers; VI: 28 engineers; VII: 73 development engineers and technicians; VIII: 45 research chemists and technicians. Total = 459.

FACTOR ANALYSIS AS A SCIENTIFIC METHOD

An attempt was made to support the basic hypotheses of the theory by performing a factor analysis of the interrelationships among reinforcers and feelings. Factor analysis is a mathematical procedure designed to determine the number of common, underlying factors or basic dimensions that will account for, and hence explain, the pattern of intercorrelations among a set of variables. These so-called common factors should be fewer in number than the variables; otherwise, little is gained in the way of producing a simpler and briefer description of them.

A number of techniques are available for performing a factor analysis. One, the centroid process, is peculiarly well adapted to the analysis of small intercorrelation matrices and permits the factorist to examine the structure of the intercorrelation system as he performs the analysis. A second, the principal factor solution, is more exact in a mathematical sense and enjoys the advantage of being readily programmed for a computer. Obviously, large intercorrelation matrices are factored by computer techniques. The series of factor analyses presented in this chapter was done with the centroid solution, the R matrices in each case being small.

A factor pattern obtained from either solution may or may not make psychological sense. Most people using factorial procedures assume that it does not make sense and proceed to transform it mathematically into a form that does. This can be done either graphically or by analytical techniques that can be programmed for a computer. A graphic solution permits some latitude in judgment on the part of the factorist and represents something of an art. The analytical solutions satisfy rigid mathematical criteria and represent about as much art as multiplying 2×2. Both types of derived or transformed solutions purport to satisfy a set of criteria called the "criteria of simple structure," a fancy name for arranging so that any given variable is "loaded on" or correlated with the smallest number of factors possible. In this series of transformations graphic solutions were used and, hence, the factorist exercised his own judgment in the selection of a derived pattern that would make sense.

For the reader unfamiliar with factor analysis procedures, it is suggested that he consult either L. L. Thurstone's *Multiple-Factor Analysis*[2] or H. H. Harmon's *Modern Factor Analysis.*[3] The first book is the definitive work in this field and contains the rationale of the procedures as a scientific method. The second book is a relatively recent standard reference work. Neither book makes for particularly easy reading.

The method of factor analysis represents the kind of risk taking that is essential to the scientific enterprise; that is, the risk of submitting a

[2]The University of Chicago Press, Chicago, 1947.
[3]The University of Chicago Press, Chicago, 1960.

question to the test of empirical data. At the outset one has no idea of what the outcome will be. Some correlation matrices yield a workable solution, others do not, and even those that yield a solution may not produce a pattern that makes psychological sense. The outcome and its value depend entirely on the intrinsic parameters of the phenomena and the ability of the factorist to bring them out. There is nothing about the method that "forces" the data or makes it yield a sense it does not have in itself. In the present case a series of four analyses was being undertaken on data drawn from disparate groups. Since the likelihood of finding any overall or general pattern by chance is small, its emergence would add markedly to the confidence that could be placed in its reality. At the outset there was no way of knowing how valuable this approach would be and, once started, it was simply continued until a number of solutions had been obtained.

Any rectangular arrangement of numerical values or the symbolic representation thereof is called a *matrix*. These are identified here by a capital letter. Hence, the square table that shows the intercorrelations among an entire set of variables is termed an R matrix in size equal to $n \times n$, where n stands for the number of variables. The rectangular arrangement of numbers that shows the correlations between each variable and each factor is termed an F matrix. It is of size $n \times m$, where n stands for the number of variables and m is the number of factors. Any column in such a matrix is termed a *column vector* and identifies one of the factors or dimensions.

This report identifies the several factors derived from the original centroid factor solutions by the symbols $C_1, C_2, C_3 \ldots$ and the factors obtained after the transformation process as $T_1, T_2, T_3 \ldots$. The relationships between the variables and the factors are called *patterns*, and for each factor solution the initial C pattern and a terminal T pattern are shown, together with the matrix that defines the transformation of the initial pattern into the terminal pattern.

Two additional kinds of information are routinely presented in factor analysis tables. For each variable there is given the sum of the squares of the factor loadings or the correlations of the variable with the factor. This value, termed the *communality*, represents the proportion of the variability that can be accounted for or explained by the common factors. If this value is 0, none of the variability can be accounted for by the factors. It is independent of them or not correlated with them. On the other hand, if this value is 1.00 or very close to 1.00, all or nearly all of the variability is accounted for or explained by the factors. The relative magnitude of these communalities reflects the extent to which the variables have something in common or are related to each other.

The second kind of information reflects the percentage of *common* variability in the entire table of intercorrelations that can be accounted for or explained by any given factor. These values then reflect the relative strength of the factors as explanatory principles in accounting for the interrelationships among the variables.

Some mention needs to be made here of the rationale for using factor analysis procedures and of the information one would expect to gain from the use of the technique. The procedure is essentially a descriptive technique. It describes a pattern of relationships among variables in a simpler, more readily grasped fashion than do the intercorrelations themselves.

This description is of course determined in part by the particular collection of variables used in the analysis; the addition or deletion of variables will alter the pattern. Of equal significance is the fact that the pattern is also determined by the collection of people in the sample from which the intercorrelations were derived. Presumably, if we were to draw at random successive samples of people from the same population, measure their characteristics, intercorrelate these measures, and factor analyze the several resulting R matrices, the resulting factor patterns would be very similar and would vary only as a function of chance or of random errors of sampling.

FACTOR ANALYSES OF THE MOTIVATION ITEMS

An attempt was made to support the basic hypotheses of the theory of adult motivation by factoring correlation matrices representing the interrelationships among the reinforcers and feelings. The ratio of the number of times in the sample two items were checked concurrently to the geometric mean of the number of times each item was checked at all was taken as the measure of correlation. These matrices were constructed from data on four groups of men in order to get some idea of the extent to which the factor patterns would show invariance over quite diverse samples of data.

These R matrices were factored by the centroid process, and the resulting factor matrices were transformed into matrices satisfying the criteria of simple structure. The end products of these factoring operations are shown as Exhibits A-1 to A-4 in Appendix A. The four analyses are ordered roughly according to the level of job held by the men. Sample A consisted of 109 maintenance and production hourly workers in a small manufacturing plant. Sample B consisted of 135 line production hourly workers in a modern chemical plant in a different location. Sample C consisted of 79 hourly maintenance men in the chemical plant. Finally, Sample D consisted of 44 production supervisors and managers in the same plant.

It may be seen from Exhibits A-1 to A-4 in Appendix A that the factoring operation yielded three factors for Sample A and four each for the other three samples. One might assume from this that the men in Sample A are less complex, motivationally speaking, than the other three. Sample D, the supervisor-manager sample, shows the most complex pattern in the lot, since the second factor, T_2, appears to be a mixture of task- and situation-oriented motivations.

In the case of each matrix the first factor is a general one, with loadings of some size on all variables. This general factor probably represents, among other things, a tendency on the part of men to respond either to many items or to a few; hence it measures something akin to a response set. That this general factor does contain the accomplishment pattern, however, is attested to by sizably larger loadings on those variables — that is, feelings of accomplishment and interesting work—that characterize this pattern. These rotations are orthogonal, thus insuring statistical independence of the factors as they stand. However, it is apparent that the first factor in each case, since it encompasses the other three, must be correlated with them.

At the bottom of each exhibit is a set of values that expresses the percentage of the common variance accounted for by each factor in each solution. In the case of T_1, the first factor, these values range from 66 to 80 percent. For the second factor, T_2, they vary from 6 to 15 percent and are correspondingly small as one moves to the third and fourth factors. The T_1 factor obviously accounts for the bulk of the intercorrelation among the motivation items.

Although these F matrices are interesting in their own right, they become more meaningful when they are analyzed as a set and their significance is evaluated against the relationships found in the Herzberg data. One of the ways to do this is to try to identify the factors that fit the hypotheses of the preceding chapter and see if similar patterns and relationships between feelings and conditions observed there also occur here. Exhibit 7 shows the end result of pulling together the factors identified as T_1 from each set; T_2 and T_3, similarly; and the three T_4 vectors from

EXHIBIT 7

**Summary of Factor Analyses of the Attitude
Survey Motivation Items on Four Job Groups**

	Terminal Factors			
	T_1	T_2	T_3	T_4
Feelings				
Accomplishment	XXXX	X		X
Confidence	XXX			XX
Recognition	XXXX		X	
Pride	XXXX			
Security	XXX		XXX	
Financial progress	X	XX	XXX	X
Personal growth	X	XX	XX	X
Responsibility		XXXX	XX	
Importance	X	X	XXX	XX
Acceptance		X	XXX	
Events or Conditions				
Promotion		XX	XXXX	
Permissive supervision	XXX	XXX		XXX
Interesting work	XXXX	XX		X
Supervision of others	X	XXXX	XXX	
Raise	X		XXXX	
Successful completion of a task	XXX	X		XXX
Praise	XXXX		X	X
Increased status		XX	X	X
Work of subordinates	X	XXX	X	X

Samples B, C, and D. What has been done here is simply to indicate by an X whether the particular motivation item is a component of—that is, loads significantly on—the particular factor in question. Thus it is possible for a variable to have anywhere from zero to four X's following it in a given column in the table. In the case of the T_1 column, only variables with unusually high loadings in the factor have been included.

Column T_1 in Exhibit 7 shows a clear-cut combination of variables that obviously corresponds to the accomplishment, task-oriented complex of feelings and conditions observed in the Herzberg data. Note that feelings of accomplishment, recognition, and pride accompanying interesting work and praise occur in all four samples. Feelings of confidence and security along with permissive supervision and successful completion of a task occur in three of the four. This is almost an exact duplication of the combination found in the Herzberg data.

In column T_2 of Exhibit 7 one finds a cluster that conforms, with some additions and deletions, to the social, situation-oriented set observed previously. One feeling, responsibility, accompanies supervision of others in all four samples. Permissive supervision and work of subordinates occur in three of the four samples. Feelings of financial progress and personal growth occur in two of the four, along with a promotion, interesting work, and increased status. In the original analysis, a feeling of financial progress was not a part of this pattern; and a feeling of personal growth and the condition of a promotion and increased status were stronger components. The most characteristic combination of variables identifying this kind of motivation is that of supervision of others with feelings of responsibility.

The T_3 pattern shows a clear-cut combination of conditions (a promotion, a raise, and supervision of others) associated with a diffuse combination of feelings (security, financial progress, importance, and acceptance) occurring in two samples. Note that feelings of financial progress, personal growth, and responsibility overlap in the T_2 and T_3 patterns, as do the conditions, a promotion and supervision of others. Although this T_3 pattern appears to characterize a money-status-oriented pattern, it obviously has sizable social overtones.

The T_4 pattern must be considered to be a variant of the accomplishment or task-oriented pattern, T_1. Here permissive supervision and successful completion of a task are accompanied by feelings of confidence and importance. From these data one would judge that the way to generate confidence and a feeling of importance in an employee is to give him a task that he can get closure on—that is, one he can complete to his own satisfaction—and let him do it the way he wants to.

A feeling of personal growth shows up as a component at least once in each of the four patterns but twice in the case of T_2 and T_3. Apparently, with these people there is some ambiguity in meaning attached to this item. According to the developmental hypothesis of the preceding chapter, many of these people would be considered motivationally immature and therefore incapable of responding appropriately to this item. Note also that increased status shows up twice in T_2 and once each in T_3 and T_4. This item is not checked with any marked frequency by these men; hence it tends not to correlate as highly with other items. It may represent a "bad word" and be rejected for that reason.

Though the clusterings are quite clearly delineated, a number of feelings and events show dual significance or ambiguity. This is particularly true of feelings of confidence, security, financial progress, personal growth, and responsibility. Similarly, promotion, permissive supervision, supervision of others, and successful completion of a task may reinforce different kinds of motivation. Their significance to a man can be judged only in terms of their meaning to him. Let us summarize diagrammatically the preceding material:

T_1, the accomplishment pattern, looks like this:

Interesting work Praise Permissive supervision Successful completion of a task	*leads to feelings of*	Accomplishment Confidence Recognition Pride Security

T_2, the social or situation-oriented pattern, looks like this:

Supervision of others Work of subordinates Permissive supervision	*leads to a feeling of*	Responsibility

T_3, the money-status-oriented pattern, looks like this:

A promotion A raise Supervision of others	*leads to feelings of*	Security Financial growth Importance Acceptance

T_4, the confidence pattern, looks like this:

Permissive supervision Successful completion of a task	*leads to feelings of*	Confidence Importance

These diagrams show which of the several conditions and events that occur on the job are particularly effective in reinforcing the work motivation of employees. Permissive supervision—that is, letting a person do a job his own way—is a reinforcing agent for three of the four motivation channels shown. It contributes to the reinforcement of feelings of accomplishment, responsibility, and confidence. Arranging for a person to get closure—that is, complete a task to his own satisfaction—contributes to both variants of the accomplishment motive. Giving a man the opportunity to supervise the work of others reinforces both situation-oriented men and those with money-status motivations. The interesting thing about all three factors is that they are under the direct control of the supervisor. It is within the supervisor's power to arrange a man's work so that he has autonomy, so that the tasks assigned to him are challenging but within his capabilities, and so that he has an opportunity to oversee or supervise the work of other people. But the supervisor may not be able to promote a man or give him a raise.

THE HACKMAN JOB SATISFACTION SCHEDULE

On the basis of this experience with the motivation items included in attitude surveys and the general format used in their presentation, a second questionnaire was constructed bearing the title, "The Hackman Job Satisfaction Schedule (HJSS)." This questionnaire appears as Appendix B. The format used here was altered somewhat to permit the respondent to check the degree of meaning for a given item. Two "feeling" words were also added to the list of items describing feelings produced by conditions generating dissatisfaction.

This questionnaire can be scored by combining the information contained in the factor analyses with the analysis of the Herzberg data. Three sets of items tapping, respectively, the accomplishment or task-oriented factor, the social or situation-oriented factor, and the money-status factor were identified. Although these sets overlapped in the analyses, there appeared to be some merit in making them independent. Accordingly, Items 2, 3, 6, and 7 in the first set and Items 1, 2, 3, 4, and 5 in the second set were combined as Factor A, the accomplishment factor. Items 1, 4, and 9 in the first set and 7, 8, and 10 in the second set were combined as Factor B, the social factor. Items 5 and 8 in the first set and Items 6 and 9 in the second set were combined as Factor C, the money-status factor. Scoring weights were assigned to these items in proportion to their factor loadings in the four factor analyses. The HJSS factors, together with their scoring weights, are shown in Exhibit 8.

EXHIBIT 8

Scoring System for the Job Satisfaction Schedule

Scoring Weights		HJSS Factors
Primary Cause	Less Significant	

Factor A
Events or Conditions

4	2	2. You were allowed to do a piece of work your own way.
3	1	3. Your work was interesting and challenging to you.
3	1	6. You completed a piece of work to your own satisfaction.
3	1	7. You were praised for the way you handled a piece of work.

Feelings

3	2	1. That you had really accomplished something.
3	2	2. Confident.
2	1	3. That you and your work were being recognized.
3	1	4. Proud.
3	2	5. Secure.

Factor B
Events or Conditions

3	2	1. You were promoted.
3	1	4. You were asked to supervise or oversee the work of others.
3	1	9. Your subordinates turned out a particularly fine piece of work.

Feelings

3	1	7. That you were growing and developing as a person.
3	1	8. Responsible for others and the company.
2	1	10. That you belonged or were accepted by the people you worked with.

Factor C
Events or Conditions

3	1	5. You got a raise in pay.
2	1	8. Your relative position or standing was made apparent to others.

Feelings

3	1	6. That you were making material and financial progress.
3	1	9. Important.

NOTE: The HJSS factors are based on responses to questions put by PSP in the course of testing. Their form has not been altered in any way. The data presented in this book are based on responses to the items as stated; had the wording been changed, the responses might well have been different.

Initial attempts to factor the items in the lists containing sources of dissatisfaction and feelings accompanying them met with little success. A centroid solution could be derived, but this centroid factor pattern could not be transformed into one with a meaningful simple structure. These data later yielded to a somewhat different treatment, described in Chapter 9. Initially, however, these two sections were scored as a *negative* factor by assigning weights proportional to the communalities of the items.

The maximum score obtainable on Factor A, the accomplishment set, is 27; on Factor B, the social set, 17; and on Factor C, the money-status set, 11. The maximum score obtainable on the negative factor, Factor N, is 85.

The hypotheses contained in the motivation model suggested that the factor scores could be treated as independent measures of motivation. We proceeded to operate on this assumption. Factor A was presumed to be a measure of task-oriented or accomplishment motivation. Factor B was considered to be a measure of situation-oriented or social motivation. Factor C was considered a measure of extrinsic or money-status motivation. Factor N was presumed to measure the extent to which a person is frustrated, angered, or made anxious by events and conditions on his job and responds emotionally to that irritation.

SUMMARY

The development of the HJSS marked the completion of the second phase of the research program. Prior to that time it had been demonstrated that the interview technique originally employed by Herzberg is a useful means of obtaining information on work reinforcers and the feelings accompanying them and that the technique in questionnaire form could be effectively adapted for use in attitude surveys.

This questionnaire adaptation yielded data that supported the hypotheses of the motivation model. The assumption of two basic kinds of motivation in employed adults was supported by the evidence. All occupational levels represented in the four samples treated in this chapter exhibited the two types of motivation: task-oriented and situation-oriented. The particular manner in which each type of motivation was reinforced varied from one occupational group to another, but certain combinations of reinforcers and feelings appeared to be invariant. Feelings of accomplishment and pride accompanied reports of interesting work and successful completion of a task; a feeling of responsibility accompanied a report of being given supervision over others.

These findings have significant implications with respect to the measurement of motivation in employed adults. A great deal of information about motivation is lost if attention is restricted to the observable behavior of an individual in response to direct stimulation. Attending to specific kinds of verbal reports—that is, of feelings accompanying reinforcing events and conditions on the job—yields direct information on the channeling of motivation. Furthermore, it clarifies the motivational significance of events and conditions—for example, a raise or a promotion—that would otherwise remain ambiguous.

Both the interview method of Herzberg and the questionnaire adaptation of it produce reports of the kind desired. But the problem is one, not of eliciting such responses, but of interpreting them. The factor analyses presented in this chapter furnish a clue as to how this problem of interpretation can be resolved. They reveal patterns of feelings and relationships existing among events and conditions on the job as well as an indication of the strength of these relationships.

In practice the HJSS has a number of limitations as an instrument for measuring individual motivation. The small number of items contributing to each factor score will produce unreliable measurement of a given individual's motivation. Following the directions, one person may describe only one episode and another may describe many. The kind of responses a person can and will give depends on the amount of work experience he has had. A person with no work experience is not in a position to respond meaningfully.

Given these limitations, it is obvious that the HJSS should not be considered an "end product." It is primarily a research instrument designed to serve as an intermediate or "bridge" device, making it possible to extend the investigation of the aforementioned relationships to other occupational groups in order to verify them. Most important, it permits deepening the investigation by determining the functional tie-in of the relationships with personality and temperament traits. The next chapter describes efforts to link the four factors of the HJSS to general personality characteristics. This was a critical step with respect to both the development of an instrument for describing individual motivation and the elucidation of a general theory of adult motivation.

4

Personality and Temperament Traits of Work–Motivated Men

IN PREPARATION for the third phase of the work-motivation research, the Hackman Job Satisfaction Schedule (HJSS) was administered routinely to men seen by Psychological Service of Pittsburgh for psychological appraisal during a period of two years. These men filled out the HJSS in conjunction with a battery of other psychological tests, and their responses were considered by the interviewer in talking with individuals to explore motivation and work experience.

In this fashion, a usable sample of 646 men was obtained. Of these 646 men, 51 percent were college graduates; an additional 21 percent had one or more years of graduate work; and 24 percent were high school graduates with or without additional formal training. Of those with training beyond the high school level, 41 percent had attended large state universities; 26 percent, small liberal arts colleges; and 20 percent, large private universities. The remainder had attended technical, business, or military schools.

These men were working for various types of companies, with heavy metals firms heading the list. Other organizations sizably represented were manufacturing concerns, chemical companies, tire and rubber producers, gas and electric utilities, security exchanges, retailers, and city, county, and federal agencies. Approximately 92 percent of the sample consisted of salaried people, and the most frequently represented job types were executives, managers, engineers, salesmen, supervisors, accountants, attorneys, sales engineers, buyers, chemists, staff assistants, production men, office workers, and public relations men.

To summarize, the sample consisted of 646 salaried men holding managerial, technical, sales, and production jobs. In the main, they were educated at the level of a bachelor's degree or somewhat beyond, and they worked in a variety of organizations. They varied in age between 25 and 45, with less representation in the younger and older age groups.

With the data on this large sample of employed men, we were in a position to extend our knowledge of the significance of the HJSS descriptions of motivation. Two supplementary kinds of information promised to be of value for this purpose. The first consisted of personal data—material drawn from the family, school, and job histories of the men. For a variety of reasons, an analysis of these data was deferred in favor of considering the second kind of information: responses to items in a self-descriptive personality inventory. The inventory selected was the Guilford-Zimmerman Temperament Survey (G-ZTS), a questionnaire with which the PSP staff has had considerable experience and which appears to tap the motivation of the respondent. Each man in the sample had taken the G-ZTS at the time of completion of the HJSS.

THE GUILFORD-ZIMMERMAN TEMPERAMENT SURVEY

The Guilford-Zimmerman Temperament Survey[1] was developed after extensive research with personality test items and used factorial methods for deriving internally consistent scales. There are ten scales based on thirty items each. Eight of the ten scales tap aspects of an individual's reaction toward, and interaction with, other people. Several of

[1]For a description of this questionnaire see either J. P. Guilford, *Personality*, McGraw-Hill, New York, 1959, pp. 184-187, or *The Guilford-Zimmerman Temperament Survey Manual of Instructions and Interpretations*, Sheridan Supply Co., Beverly Hills, 1949.

them have direct implications for motivation measurement, and two involve characteristics generally regarded as temperament traits.

A factor analysis of the G-ZTS scales reported by A. W. Bendig[2] and based on data on employed adult men in PSP's files demonstrated the existence of three factors in these scales. The first factor loaded on G (general activity), A (ascendance), and S (sociability); the second, on E (emotional stability), O (objectivity), F (friendliness), and P (personal relations); and the third on R (restraint) and T (thoughtfulness). The tenth scale, M (masculinity), showed no clear-cut relationship with these factors. The third factor might be identified as a temperament trait. The other two factors clearly relate to the motivation model. The first factor taps the positive aspect of the motivation process; the second taps the negative aspect of this process.

It should be pointed out here that the individual *items* and not the scale scores were to be related to the HJSS factor scores. Interest in the G-ZTS was confined to the total pool of 300 carefully screened items and not to the interpretation placed on them by other investigators.

PRELIMINARY ITEM ANALYSES OF THE G-ZTS

On the basis of experience with the IIJSS, it was decided to work initially with the A and B factors as basic descriptions of the motivations of employed adults. It was assumed that the A factor, the task-oriented or accomplishment pattern, would be most characteristic of the motivation of salaried men and, indeed, widely distributed throughout the working population. The B factor, the situation-oriented or social pattern, on the other hand, would appear to be most characteristic of men with supervisory or management jobs and, perhaps, not so widely distributed. The elements of C, the money-status pattern, would be least characteristic of salaried men and possibly less widely distributed in a working population. The A and B factors give insight into what it is about a job that is rewarding to a man. Relating these two factors to the results of an inventory like the G-ZTS should yield added insight into what people are like who derive their satisfaction from these kinds of reinforcements.

[2]"Age Differences in the Inter-scale Factor Structure of the Guilford-Zimmerman Temperament Survey," *Journal of Consulting Psychology*, Vol. 24, 1960, pp. 134-138.

On the basis of these assumptions, the *first step* in the analysis was to isolate four samples of cases from the large HJSS supply. One sample consisted of people scoring high on both the A and B factors. A second sample was composed of men scoring low on both factors. A third sample comprised men scoring high on A and low on B. Finally, a fourth sample consisted of men scoring low on A and high on B. High and low were arbitrarily determined by setting nonoverlapping cutting scores on the factor-score continua. For example, scores between 23 and 27 were considered high on Factor A; 0 to 18 were considered low. Scores of 15 to 17 were considered high on Factor B; 0 to 9 were considered low. No attention was paid to the remainder of the factor pattern, except that it was apparent that high C scores tended to go with high A and B scores.

It was encouraging to find that the distribution of yes and no responses to individual items on the G-ZTS significantly differentiated among these four groups, but one finding was not anticipated: that the bulk of these items differentiated between high B and low B people. It was discovered that many of the responses to G-ZTS items differentiated as well between high A and low A people as they did between high B and low B people. In other words, the task-oriented and the situation-oriented men could not be effectively distinguished.

The *second step* in the analysis examined those cases remaining after the four extreme A and B groups were eliminated. From this set two samples were generated, one consisting of men with high N scores (40 and above) and the other of men with low N scores (9 and below). Comparisons of distributions of yes and no responses to individual items on the G-ZTS between these two groups showed significant differentiation on a large number of items. These items tended to be of a type different from those noted in the A and B analyses described earlier.

At this point PSP had removed from the sample cases those that were high on both A and B factors, low on both A and B factors, high on one and low on the other, and high on the N factor and low on it. The *third step* in these preliminary analyses was to generate four additional samples. These consisted of (1) those groups of cases whose scores were in the center of the range on A and either high or low on B and (2) those in the center of the range on B and either high or low on A. For each of these four groups PSP determined the number of men who responded yes or no to each item on the G-ZTS.

By judiciously combining these groups it was possible to develop larger samples of cases in which high A men could be contrasted with low A men with a partial statistical control of the effects of also being high or low on the B factor. By letting A_1 stand for a high A group, A_2 for a group whose scores were intermediate, and A_3 for those whose A scores were low (with similar notation for the B groupings), the scheme for contrasting high A-low A and high B-low B groups shown in Exhibit 9 was developed.

EXHIBIT 9

Structure of the High A-Low A and High B-Low B Comparisons

	Criterion Group	No. Cases	Criterion Group	No. Cases	Criterion Group	No. Cases	Criterion Group	No. Cases
	A_1B_1	58	A_3B_1	31	A_1B_1	58	A_1B_3	36
	A_1B_2	49	A_3B_2	49	A_2B_1	56	A_2B_3	59
	A_1B_3	36	A_3B_3	51	A_3B_1	31	A_3B_3	51
Totals	A_1B	143	A_3B	131	$A.B_1$	145	$A.B_3$	146

Differences in the distributions of yes and no responses made by the combined A_1 versus A_3 groups and the combined B_1 versus B_3 groups were tested for significance by means of chi-square. This is a standard procedure for evaluating frequency differences of this kind. Chi-square is used here, and in subsequent analyses, as a method of item analysis. It gives an indication of the extent to which differences in the frequency of occurrence of yes and no responses in the high A or B groups, in contrast to those in the low A or B groups, should be considered real phenomena or attributed to chance variation. A description of the method may be found in McNemar's *Psychological Statistics* or any other standard reference work in statistics.

The number of items in the G-ZTS that are significantly related to the motivation factor scores on the HJSS are shown in Exhibit 10. Note that the number of items significant at each of three levels is broken down by the G-ZTS scale and that the M Scale, a measure of masculinity, does not appear. Few of these M items were significantly related to the factor scores, and their nature suggests that they are tapping something other than work motivation.

EXHIBIT 10

Number of Items at Set Levels of Significance
on Each of the G-ZTS Scales for the A Factor and B Factor Comparisons

| G-ZTS Scale | High A vs. Low A | | | | High B vs. Low B | | | |
| | Level of Significance | | | | Level of Significance | | | |
	.05	.01	.001	Total	.05	.01	.001	Total
G (General Activity)	0	5	0	5	3	8	4	15
R (Restraint)	2	0	0	2	5	1	0	6
A (Ascendance)	2	1	2	5	3	3	5	11
S (Sociability)	3	2	0	5	5	3	3	11
E (Emotional Stability)	1	1	1	3	4	0	0	4
O (Objectivity)	6	0	0	6	2	1	0	3
F (Friendliness)	2	2	0	4	6	1	0	7
T (Thoughtfulness)	6	1	2	9	1	1	1	3
P (Personal Relations)	1	0	0	1	2	1	4	7
Totals	23	12	5	40	31	19	17	67

It is apparent from Exhibit 10 that many more items contribute to the high B versus low B differentiation than to the high A versus low A differentiation, a somewhat surprising finding considering the frequency with which these men check the elements of the accomplishment pattern. It is also apparent that certain scales, notably G, A, and S, appear to contain a disproportionate number of motivation-related items.

PSP was encouraged by its success in identifying items which distinguish between men with high and low A and B factor scores on the HJSS. However, it was noted that out of the 40 items differentiating between high and low A people, 14 also appeared as differentiating between high and low B people. The analysis was not distinguishing between the two types of motivation as neatly as one would like.

DEFINITIVE ITEM ANALYSES OF THE G-ZTS

The final attempts to sharpen this differentiation proceeded as follows: From the original sample of HJSS cases, those already used in the high negative factor (N) and the low negative factor comparison were eliminated. All cases were then identified in which the A factor was 23 to 27 inclusive (a high A group) and in which the A factor was 0 to 18 inclusive, (a low A group). An attempt was made to match each case in the high A list with a low A case in which the B, C, and N factor scores varied by no more than four points. In this fashion 120 cases were identified, 60 in the high A group and 60 in the low A group. Examination of the distribution of factor scores on these two samples showed nonoverlapping distributions on the A factor and completely overlapping distributions on B, C, and N factors.

These 120 cases were then returned to the supply. The next step was to perform a similar set of operations to obtain matched samples of high and low B cases. B factor scores between 15 and 17 were defined as high and those between 0 and 9 as low. In this fashion 180 cases were identified, 90 in the high group and 90 in the low group. No statistically significant differences could be observed between the two groups on the A, C, and N factors.

These 180 cases were then returned to the supply and a similar identification of matched high and low C cases was made. The two matched C groups were composed of 142 cases, 71 in each group. The cutting score criteria here were 8 to 11 inclusive for the high group and 0 to 6 inclusive for the low group.

The design then for the item analyses of the items on Scales G, R, A, S, E, O, F, P, and T of the G-ZTS was as follows:

Factor	Low Group	High Group
A	60	60
B	90	90
C	71	71

The 106 cases in the high N-low N factor item analyses do not appear in these three comparisons. However, these high and low N groups were indifferently matched on the A factor and the B factor and were not matched at all on the C factor. Also, a case could appear in each of the A, B, and C factor comparisons. These three paired samples were not independent in the ordinary sense of the word, and one might expect some correlation among the item analyses performed on each of the three pairs of groups.

Appendix C lists the items from each G-ZTS scale which show significant statistical differentiation. Those items are arranged by the motivation subset to which they are assigned. The response more characteristic of the high A, B, C, or N factor group is given together with an indication of the level of significance.

Of the 270 items in the G-ZTS subjected to analysis, 160 show a relationship to the HJSS factor scores. All told, 30 items show a significant relationship with HJSS Factor A; 66, with Factor B; 29, with Factor C; and 64, with Factor N. A total of 29 items show a significant relationship with 2 factors, 3 items are significantly related to 3 factors, and the remaining 131 items are related to a single factor.

THE DEVELOPMENT OF PSYCHOLOGICALLY MEANINGFUL MOTIVATION SCALES

Worthy of note is the extent to which items related to particular factor scores come from particular G-ZTS scales. Items related to Factor A come from all scales, but most frequently from the thoughtfulness scale of the G-ZTS. Items related to Factor B also come from all scales but are heavily concentrated in the general activity and ascendance scales. Items related to Factor C come from the restraint, sociability, and friendliness scales, although they are also found in all other scales except emotional stability and personal relations. Items related to the N factor come primarily from the emotional stability, objectivity, friendliness, thoughtfulness, personal relations, and general activity scales, in that order of frequency.

Even a superficial examination of the item subsets related to each of the factors reveals their relative homogeneity. Factor A items tend to be similar to one another and different from B, C, or N factor items. B, C, and N factor item subsets exhibit this same characteristic. Also noteworthy about this pool of items is that the items not related to any of the factors are heterogeneous with respect to the four factor subsets and heterogeneous with respect to one another. This applies to those items with reasonable variation in frequency of yes-no responses. (Some items were consistently answered yes or no.)

However, some heterogeneity could be observed within a factor subset and appeared to relate to the G-ZTS scales from which the items came. For example, 15 items in the B factor subset, all reflecting how energetically and effectively a man works, come from the G-ZTS general activity scale. No other items of this type occurred in the total pool of significant items. In the B factor subset, 11 items reflecting a type of aggressiveness in social situations came from the G-ZTS ascendance scale. Four other items in the subset, two from the sociability scale and two from the friendliness scale, were of the same type. No others like these occurred in the total sample of significant items. An examination of all four subsets suggested that smaller, more homogeneous collections of items could be isolated by attending to the G-ZTS scale from which an item came and to its manifest content. By doing so, the 66 items in the B factor subset were sorted into four more homogeneous pools of items labeled, respectively, B_1, B_2, B_3, and B_4. The 64 items in the N factor subset were assigned to one of three more homogeneous pools, and Factor A and Factor C subsets could be sorted into two more homogeneous pools each.

Eleven collections of items were identified. Exhibit 11 shows the way in which G-ZTS items were distributed into each collection. Note that B_1 contains only general activity items; B_2, predominantly ascendance items; B_3, objectivity, friendliness, and personal relations items; B_4, restraint and emotional stability items, and so on. The numbers of items in each collection varies from 11 in the case of the N_1 scale to 30 in the case of the N_2 scale.

EXHIBIT 11

Distribution of Motivation Subsets by the G-ZTS Scale

G-ZTS Scale	Motivation Subset										
	B_1	B_2	B_3	B_4	C_1	C_2	A_1	A_2	N_1	N_2	N_3
G	15					3	3		7		
R			1	7	4	1	3	1	1	4	
A		11		1		3		3		2	
S		2	1	2	6		2			1	
E				5			2		3	11	
O			4	1	3	1		4		4	7
F		2	4		2	4	1	3			9
T				3	2			7		8	
P			7					1			7
Totals	15	15	17	19	17	12	11	19	11	30	23

Although there is always some danger in specifying the content of a set of items by the use of descriptive adjectives, each set has been identified with one or more adjectives. These words describe individuals who tend to answer all the items in the keyed direction and represent extremes of the motivational characteristics in question. Obviously, when these items are administered to a large group of people a distribution on each subset results. Some people answer all of them in the keyed direction; some, none of them; most will respond to varying numbers of them in the keyed direction.

To characterize the descriptive categories into which these items are distributed, the scale designates are listed together with the adjective or adjectives that might be used to describe a person who answered the bulk of the items in the indicated fashion:

B_1 — energetic, vigorous, industrious
B_2 — socially aggressive, dynamic, competitive
B_3 — sympathetic, friendly, tolerant
B_4 — serious minded, organized, confident, ambitious
C_1 — deferent, admiring, sociable
C_2 — assertive, authoritative, domineering
A_1 — hyperactive
A_2 — egocentric, introspective
N_1 — spiritless, lethargic
N_2 — anxiety ridden, apprehensive
N_3 — aggressive, pugnacious, resentful

INTERPRETATION OF THE SUBSETS

Two subsets are tied directly to work, since they contain references to work in the items. The set identified as B_1 describes how energetically, industriously, and efficiently a man works. By contrast, B_4 describes a work style. B_2, B_3, C_1, and C_2 describe types of social role playing, the first three in a group setting and the fourth in a face-to-face setting. A_1 differs from B_1 in that no direction or channeling of energy is implied. N_1 denies the characteristics described in B_1. C_2 differs from B_2 in that it describes a type of aggressiveness in social situations that does not have the general social approval given to B_2. A_2 tends to deny what is represented in B_3 and C_1. N_2 denies the characteristics delineated in B_4, and N_3 denies the characteristics described in B_3.

Some readily anticipated conclusions and other rather unexpected ones follow from relating the characteristics described by these 11 subsets to the HJSS factors with which they are associated.

The HJSS A factor, or what is termed the accomplishment or task-oriented factor, describes a man who gets his reinforcement on the job from having interesting and challenging work, successfully completing a task, being allowed to work under his own direction, and receiving praise. He characterizes himself on the motivation scales as hyperactive, with little or no channeling or direction to his activity, and as highly egocentric. Remembering that in this analysis other types of reinforcement are controlled out, perhaps this description is to be expected. Certainly this type of motivation untempered by other motives may characterize a *closure-seeker* or, in most extreme form, a *perfectionist*. Rarely in industry would we expect to find this type of motivation in pure form.

The HJSS B factor, or what is termed the social or situation-oriented factor, describes a man who gets his reinforcement on the job from being given supervisory responsibility and a promotion and from having his subordinates turn out a good piece of work. On the motivation scales he describes himself as energetic and industrious; socially aggressive and competitive; sympathetic and tolerant of others; serious minded, confident, and ambitious. We might call him a "24-hour-a-day" man. Certainly he describes himself in terms of all the positive characteristics industry would like to see in a supervisor or manager.

The HJSS C factor, or what is termed the money-status factor, describes a man who is getting his reinforcement from things extrinsic to the work he is doing—from increases in pay and increases in status. A "pure" C man is denying that the work he does and his interaction with other people on the job are primary sources of satisfaction to him. Such a man sees himself on the motivation scales as respectful, admiring, and sociable as well as assertive, authoritative, and domineering. Although these two patterns appear to be incompatible, they probably represent two forms of social role playing that he turns on or off at will. An effective social role player is either deferent or dominant, depending on the situation in which he finds himself. The ability to play both roles well is required of most men in the salaried industrial hierarchy. This man appears to be a manipulator of people; his primary satisfaction comes from the development and exercise of social skills that can be used to manipulate others.

The HJSS N factor, or what we have termed the emotional factor, describes a man who reacts negatively and emotionally to practically everything connected with his work and his job. Dissatisfaction and unhappiness on the job are a way of life for him. On the motivation scales he classifies himself as spiritless and lacking in energy, anxiety ridden and apprehensive, pugnacious and resentful. The first of these three descriptions denies the energy characteristic appearing in B and also in A. The second typifies the person who is running scared, perhaps to the point where fear interferes with any form of useful activity. The third depicts a person who responds with anger and aggression to most things that go on around him. He is a hard man to live with on the job.

The four B scales and the two C scales appear to describe adaptive motivational characteristics, in the sense that men with these characteristics would be expected to be successful in most work settings. The two A scales describe characteristics that might or might not be adaptive in given jobs. The three N scales appear to be getting at nonadaptive characteristics, at least in most types of jobs. This is particularly true of N_1 and N_2, but there are probably some jobs in which the N_3 characteristic would aid and abet success.

SUMMARY

The development of these 11 motivation subsets established the desired linkage between the four factors of the HJSS and general personality characteristics. Though it was now possible to describe the personal characteristics of men attuned to a particular kind of reinforcement on the job, the reliability and value of this linkage remained largely hypothetical. It remained to be determined whether the subsets were reliable in a statistical sense; that is, were useful for measuring purposes. Our sample consisted of salaried men; it might be suspected that these item responses would characterize this group but not women or men employed at hourly rates. Essentially, it remained to be demonstrated whether the indicated characteristics related in any significant way in such factors as type of job, position in the occupational hierarchy, work performance, effectiveness, and so forth.

These questions formed the central concerns of the third phase of the research. They are taken up systematically in the following chapters, beginning with the statistical and differential properties of scales built from the subsets and progressing to their predictive validity—the extent to which they are related to job performance.

5

Statistical and Differential Properties of the Motivation Scales

THIS CHAPTER DESCRIBES FINDINGS with respect to the range of differences shown by men and women in various types of jobs on the personal characteristics tapped by 11 motivation scales derived from the Guilford-Zimmerman Temperament Survey. Findings for 17 job groups are presented, some composed of men and some of women, ranging through various levels of the occupational hierarchy. The composition of these groups is later described in detail, but it may be noted here that this collection of samples, comprising a total N of 1709, includes only a few of the 646 men used in determining the scales, as described in the previous chapter. Thus they form a separate and independent application of the motivation scales.

At this point we have sets of items referring to personal characteristics rather than scales in the true sense. To approach the problem of describing group differences and interrelationships, these sets of items must be converted to scales so that each person's responses can be expressed as a simple form of measurement. As soon as this is done, it should be determined whether these measures are reliable; in other words, whether the items constituting a given scale are consistent with one another on the basis of actual responses and whether the scale as a whole yields consistent results on repeated applications. The following sections therefore take up the development of a scoring system for the motivation scales and the statistical reliability of the scales.

THE MOTIVATION SCALES

A scoring system for the items in each of the sets was devised as follows: An item differentiating between any pair of matched HJSS factor groups at the .05 level of significance was assigned a weight of 1; an item differentiating at the .01 level of significance was assigned a weight of 2; and a weight of 3 was assigned to an item differentiating at the .001 level of significance. By the use of this system a maximum score could be obtained on each of the scales according to the following schedule:

B_1—22	C_1—20	A_1—16	N_1—15
B_2—23	C_2—16	A_2—22	N_2—51
B_3—23			N_3—38
B_4—27			

To give some idea of the range of individual differences in response to these scales, Exhibit 12 records the scores corresponding to the 5th, 50th, and 95th percentile ranks — that is, the scores below which 5, 50, and 95 percent of a group of 564 men fell. These men came from the sample of appraisal cases used in the original HJSS factor score analyses.

Although it is not entirely apparent from this exhibit, there are wide individual differences in the way men describe themselves on these scales. On B_1, for example, the measure of how vigorously and effectively a man works, at least one man denied having this characteristic entirely and a number checked all the items on the scale in the keyed direction. The maximum score occurred at least once in the case of Scales B_1, B_2, B_3, C_2, A_1, and N_1, and one less than the maximum occurred in the case of Scales B_4, C_1, and A_2. Minimum scores occurred in Scales B_1, N_1, N_2, N_3;

EXHIBIT 12

5th, 50th, and 95th Percentiles
on the G-ZTS Motivation Scales

| | Percentiles | | |
Scale	5th	50th	95th
B_1	5	16	22
B_2	7	16	22
B_3	8	16	21
B_4	11	18	23
C_1	5	11	16
C_2	3	8	13
A_1	2	8	14
A_2	6	13	18
N_1	0	1	8
N_2	4	17	32
N_3	0	9	23

one more than the minimum occurred in Scales B_2, C_2, A_1, and A_2. (This kind of information should be reassuring to those who fear that people have such strong tendencies to answer items of this type in a socially approved fashion that they cannot describe themselves honestly on them.)

Scales B_1, B_2, B_3, and B_4 tend to be negatively skewed; that is, the scores tend to be distributed toward the high end of the scales. By contrast, Scales N_1, N_2, and N_3 tend to be positively skewed; that is, the scores tend to concentrate at the low ends of these scales. The two C scales and the two A scales show symmetrical distributions.

RELIABILITIES OF THE SCALES

An immediate question that arises when an instrument purports to measure anything concerns its reliability. The reliability question divides naturally into two parts — the first asking whether the items constituting a given scale are consistent with one another and the second asking whether the scale as a whole yields consistent results on repeated application. In the simple nonpsychological case of using a ruler, for example, the first question requires that all the units of the ruler be units of length (the matter of their equality involves the more advanced question of "scaling") and the second requires that using the ruler repeatedly to measure the same object yields the same result. In psychological measurement the question of interitem consistency translates into "split-half reliability" and that of the results of repeated measurements translates into "test-retest reliability." Other things being equal, one would expect the coefficients of split-half reliability to be higher than the coefficients of test-retest reliability because the former are based on responses concurrent in time.

Split-Half Reliabilities of the Individual Scales

Each set of items on each scale was randomly split into two subsets of equal size, with minor adjustments to make the subset score maximums equivalent. A random sample of 116 cases was drawn from the large sample of 564 cases. Two scores were obtained on each scale, one from each of the two random subsets. These paired scores were then correlated, with the result shown in Exhibit 13.

EXHIBIT 13

**Split-Half Reliabilities of
G-ZTS Motivation Scales**

Scale	r_{ab}	r_{xx}
B_1	.59	.75
B_2	.64	.78
B_3	.52	.69
B_4	.43	.60
C_1	.35	.52
C_2	.24	.38
A_1	.44	.61
A_2	.55	.71
N_1	.51	.68
N_2	.66	.80
N_3	.60	.75

Two sets of reliability coefficients are shown here, one (r_{ab}) obtained as just described. The second set represents the coefficients corrected or adjusted by the Spearman-Brown prophecy formula, which indicates what the reliability coefficient should be for a pool of items twice as large as the one used in the original calculation. These are the coefficients (r_{xx}) that should be attended to in interpreting the reliabilities of the scales.

These latter coefficients vary in size from .38 in the case of the C_2 scale to .80 in the case of the N_2 scale. This variation is, in part, a reflection of the fact that only 12 items make up the C_2 set, whereas 30 items make up the N_2 set. Although coefficients of this type in the neighborhood of .90 or higher are very desirable for scales purporting to describe traits or characteristics of single individuals, coefficients of this order of magnitude suffice for the description of groups and for investigating the relationships that exist among the individual scales.

Test-Retest Reliabilities of the Individual Scales

An examination of PSP's case files identified 92 appraisal cases with two sets of motivation scale scores, one obtained at the time of a first administration and one at the time of a second. The periods of time elapsing between the two varied from six months to four years. The conditions surrounding the cases were essentially the same at the time of the two appraisals. In addition, 22 cases were identified in which a man was seen initially as a counseling case and later as an appraisal case. These cases are reported in Chapter 9.

For these 92 cases two types of analysis were performed. First, the correlations between the first and second administration of the questionnaire were computed for each scale. These are the test-retest reliability coefficients that reflect the consistency of self-description across a time interval. To examine the hypothesis that there would be consistent increases or decreases in scores on some scales with elapsed time, the average scale scores were computed on first and second administration. Exhibit 14 shows the end product of these analyses.

Attending first to the question of whether significant shifts in these scale scores occur, the data in Exhibit 14 definitely suggest that there is no such set of consistent shifts. The paired means on each scale are close together in value. The largest difference is .9 and the smallest is .1; none is statistically significant. Shifts in these scale scores within individuals are not consistently upward or downward.

EXHIBIT 14

Relationship Between First and Second Administrations
of the G-ZTS Scored|for the Motivation Scales
(92 Appraisal Cases)

Motivation Scale	Mean, First Administration	Mean, Second Administration	Test-Retest Reliability
B_1	14.2	14.5	.63
B_2	13.7	14.4	.68
B_3	16.9	16.1	.46
B_4	17.1	17.0	.52
C_1	10.9	10.8	.39
C_2	8.2	8.0	.68
A_1	8.0	7.4	.65
A_2	13.0	12.4	.65
N_1	2.8	2.6	.52
N_2	19.4	18.5	.69
N_3	11.7	11.0	.76

That sizable shifts in scale scores from one time to another do occur is attested to by the magnitude of the test-retest reliability coefficients. These vary from .39 to .76. They are, as a group, roughly of the same order of magnitude as the split-half coefficients shown in Exhibit 13. It is apparent that these scales are getting at a set of consistent characteristics in these men, but characteristics that can and do vary from one time to another. Any developmental hypothesis regarding motivation would of course be difficult to substantiate if these coefficients were all in the neighborhood of .90 to .95, since no significant average shifts occurred from first to second administration. These data, however, shed little light on whether significant changes in these characteristics in particular individuals occur over time.

DIFFERENCES ACROSS JOB GROUPS

One of the ways in which the meaning attached to the motivation scales may give insight into the characteristics of motivated adults is to examine a variety of groups of adults in order to see whether the scales are sensitive enough to detect differences and whether consistent differences occur across groups. Motivation scale data are available on a number of groups of men and women. Some of these are small, intact work groups that were seen either for the purpose of description and, ultimately, management development or for the purpose of establishing standards to be used in the selection of future employees in the same type of job.

In some cases the groups represent people seen by PSP for selection who were hired by the company and were still in its employ. Some groups consist of all applicants for particular jobs who were seen but not necessarily hired. Some groups are composed of men, others of women. Some hold salaried jobs, others hourly jobs. Some are women college students, others male college students.

The intent in describing these groups is not to furnish accurate descriptions of occupational types on these scales. Rather, it is intended to demonstrate the sensitivity of the system and to furnish data on the basis of which, using common-sense criteria, the significance of the characteristics being measured by the individual scales can be evaluated.

Exhibits 15 through 25, one for each of the scales, show the middle 50 percent of the distribution of scores for each of 17 groups of men and women. In these exhibits the two extreme points of the horizontal lines represent the 25th and 75th percentiles; that is, the points below which 25 percent and 75 percent, respectively, of the samples fall. The perpendicular lines are the medians or 50th percentiles of the groups. The length of the lines is of course a reflection of the amount of variability in each group. Some groups are composed of people very much alike on a given scale; others are quite heterogeneous. The positions of the medians relative to the two end points give information on the degree and direction of asymmetry in the distributions.

Composition of the 17 Groups

In these exhibits the ten groups listed at the top of each are composed of men; the seven at the bottom of each are composed entirely of women. Two groups are made up of college students who had not as yet entered the job market. The group of 453 management trainee applicants consisted of college seniors coming from a variety of educational institutions who were applying for management trainee positions in a large basic metals company. The group of 116 women college students is a 25 percent random sample of 17- and 18-year-old college freshmen to whom the G-ZTS had been routinely administered as a part of their orientation program. These students attend a denominational women's college in the Northeast.

A number of these groups represent 100 percent samples of men and women examined either by PSP or by personnel officers in their own companies for the purpose of setting selection standards. Included here are groups of 37 securities salesmen, 34 bank officers, and 37 women bank tellers. Several of the groups were seen by PSP for descriptive purposes in connection with personnel surveys. These include 85 research and development managers, 80 U.S. Government executives attending a management seminar, and 37 public school administrators and teachers.

In the case of some of these samples, the men or women were seen as applicants for specific jobs or for advancement into higher-level positions. The G-ZTS was administered either by PSP or under its direction. The motivation scales were not available at the time the selection decisions were made.

These groups include 73 public utility operators, 120 hourly production workers in a manufacturing plant, 102 hourly industrial laborers seen for potential for a different kind of work, 322 women applicants for picker jobs at a mushroom farm, and 57 registered nurses being seen for head nurse positions. The group of 32 professional women was composed mainly of teachers and administrators in a public school system. The 101 women secretaries and 60 women clerical workers represent appraisal cases in PSP files who were seen for a variety of reasons.

Variation Among Job Groups

Exhibit 15 shows the distribution of 17 groups of men and women on the B_1 scale. This scale reflects how energetically and industriously an individual works. If one were to generalize across the samples of men in comparison to the samples of women, he would probably judge that the men have somewhat more of this characteristic than do the women. However, four of the groups of women compare quite favorably with the men in this characteristic. There is a fairly marked tendency for these hourly men to describe themselves as less energetic than the salaried men. However, this is not typical of the hourly women. The distribution of scores on the 322 women picker applicants compares favorably with the salaried women and with the men in general.

EXHIBIT 15

**Middle 50 Percent of the Distributions of
Selected Job and Student Groups — B_1 Scale**

Securities Salesmen

Industrial Salesmen

R & D Managers

U.S. Government Executives

Bank Officers

Public School Administrators and Teachers

Public Utility Operators

Management Trainee Applicants

Hourly Workers

Hourly Industrial Laborers

Professional Women

Women Secretaries

Women Picker Applicants

Women Bank Tellers

Women Clerical Workers

Registered Nurses

Women College Students

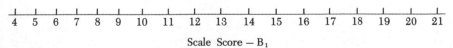

4   5   6   7   8   9   10   11   12   13   14   15   16   17   18   19   20   21

Scale Score — B_1

As might be expected, the two groups of salesmen and the research and development managers tend to score high on the scale, while the group of women college students tends to run quite low. It is of interest to note that the U.S. Government executives and the public school administrators and teachers describe themselves as possessing this characteristic and compare favorably with the industrial men. The 75th percentile for the group of government executives is the second highest in the entire set.

Exhibit 16 shows the distributions of the middle 50 percent of these groups on the B_2 scale. This scale describes the socially aggressive, dynamic, competitive person in our society. It is apparent that these men, particularly the salaried men, are much more likely to think of themselves as having this characteristic than are these women. The securities salesmen as a group score high on this scale and are quite homogeneous with respect to it. The research and development managers and applicants for management training show this characteristic to a marked degree. By contrast, the three groups of hourly paid men tend to deny having this characteristic and respond in a way similar to the salaried women.

The women clerical workers, together with the women college students, show this kind of social aggressiveness less frequently than do the salaried women or men in the hourly paid groups.

Exhibit 17 shows the distributions of the middle 50 percent of these groups on Scale B_3. This scale describes the tolerant, sympathetic, friendly person. In contrast to the two preceding scales, this characteristic does not particularly differentiate among the job groups. Differences between salaried and hourly groups are notable for their absence, particularly among the employed men. The one differentiation, perhaps unexpected, that can be observed here is the partial denial of the characteristic by the two groups of college students. Neither the college men (management trainee applicants) nor the college women describe themselves as having this characteristic well developed.

On the basis of present evidence, it is impossible to judge whether this latter finding represents a developmental shift in a motivational characteristic from a relatively young adult age to greater maturity. It could be hypothesized equally well that a selection factor operates in industry to eliminate those who continue to be intolerant, unsympathetic, and unfriendly. These data pose a problem to be solved by future research.

Exhibit 18 shows the distribution of the middle 50 percent of people in these job groups on the B_4 scale. This scale describes the serious-minded,

(text continues on page 70)

EXHIBIT 16

Middle 50 Percent of the Distributions of
Selected Job and Student Groups — B₂ Scale

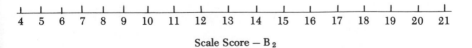

Securities Salesmen

Industrial Salesmen

Management Trainee Applicants

Public School Administrators and Teachers

R & D Managers

Bank Officers

U.S. Government Executives

Public Utility Operators

Hourly Industrial Laborers

Hourly Workers

Professional Women

Women Secretaries

Registered Nurses

Women Bank Tellers

Women College Students

Women Picker Applicants

Women Clerical Workers

| 4 | 5 | 6 | 7 | 8 | 9 | 10 | 11 | 12 | 13 | 14 | 15 | 16 | 17 | 18 | 19 | 20 | 21 |

Scale Score — B₂

EXHIBIT 17

Middle 50 Percent of the Distributions of
Selected Job and Student Groups — B₃ Scale

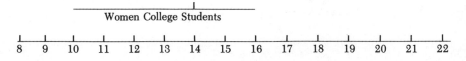

Securities Salesmen

R&D Managers

Public Utility Operators

Bank Officers

Industrial Salesmen

Public School Administrators and Teachers

U.S. Government Executives

Hourly Workers

Hourly Industrial Laborers

Management Trainee Applicants

Professional Women

Women Secretaries

Women Bank Tellers

Registered Nurses

Women Picker Applicants

Women Clerical Workers

Women College Students

```
8   9   10  11  12  13  14  15  16  17  18  19  20  21  22
```

Scale Score — B₃

EXHIBIT 18

**Middle 50 Percent of the Distributions of
Selected Job and Student Groups —B₄ Scale**

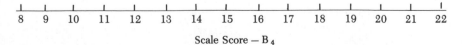

R&D Managers

Bank Officers

Securities Salesmen

Public School Administrators and Teachers

Industrial Salesmen

Hourly Workers

U.S. Government Executives

Management Trainee Applicants

Hourly Industrial Laborers

Public Utility Operators

Professional Women

Women Secretaries

Registered Nurses

Women Bank Tellers

Women Picker Applicants

Women Clerical Workers

Women College Students

| 8 | 9 | 10 | 11 | 12 | 13 | 14 | 15 | 16 | 17 | 18 | 19 | 20 | 21 | 22 |

Scale Score — B₄

confident, ambitious person who is responsible and conscientious in his work style — the "24-hour-a-day man."

It is immediately apparent that the college women are most atypical, claiming substantially less of this characteristic than the other job groups. There is a consistent tendency for the women at the lower end of the occupational hierarchy to describe themselves as possessing less of this trait than the women at the upper end — the secretaries and professional women showing scores comparable to those of the men. A similar trend is evident in the distribution of the samples of men, with the research and development managers, bank officers, securities salesmen, and public school administrators and teachers setting the upper levels of the distribution. There is a notable discrepancy between the college women and the college men in this sample.

Exhibit 19 shows the distribution of the middle 50 percent of these people on Scale C_1. This scale describes the sociable, respectful, deferent person in our society. The exhibit is interesting from a number of points of view. The scale apparently does not differentiate among the seven groups of women. These tend to occupy the middle portion of the scale, suggesting that the women deny they have either none of this characteristic or a great deal of it.

The ten groups of men, on the other hand, are well distributed throughout the scale. The hourly paid men, together with the U.S. Government executives and research and development managers, describe themselves as not possessing the trait to a marked degree. The two groups of salesmen and, somewhat surprisingly, the group of teachers and administrators describe themselves as having this characteristic.

This is one of two scales built from items differentiating high money-status-oriented and low money-status-oriented people on the HJSS. The only one of these group descriptions that would probably not jibe with our ideas about what kinds of people are motivated by money and status considerations is the one characterizing teachers and administrators.

Exhibit 20 shows the distributions of the middle 50 percent of the scores for each of these groups on the C_2 scale, which describes the assertive, domineering, authoritative person in our society.

Three groups of men stand out as atypical on this scale. Both groups of salesmen and the student management trainee applicants tend to run much higher scores than do the other groups of men or women. The securities salesmen in particular are characterized by this scale. The three groups of hourly paid men tend to distribute themselves toward the low end

EXHIBIT 19

Middle 50 Percent of the Distributions of
Selected Job and Student Groups — C_1 Scale

Securities Salesmen

Industrial Salesmen

Public School Administrators and Teachers

Management Trainee Applicants

Bank Officers

Public Utility Operators

Hourly Workers

R & D Managers

Hourly Industrial Laborers

U.S. Government Executives

Professional Women

Registered Nurses

Women Bank Tellers

Women Secretaries

Women Picker Applicants

Women College Students

Women Clerical Workers

| 6 | 7 | 8 | 9 | 10 | 11 | 12 | 13 | 14 | 15 |

Scale Score — C_1

EXHIBIT 20

Middle 50 Percent of the Distributions of
Selected Job and Student Groups — C_2 Scale

Securities Salesmen

Industrial Salesmen

Management Trainee Applicants

Public School Administrators and Teachers

R & D Managers

Bank Officers

U.S. Government Executives

Public Utility Operators

Hourly Workers

Hourly Industrial Laborers

Women Bank Tellers

Women College Students

Women Picker Applicants

Registered Nurses

Professional Women

Women Secretaries

Women Clerical Workers

| 4 | 5 | 6 | 7 | 8 | 9 | 10 | 11 | 12 |

Scale Score — C_2

of the scale, even lower than the women picker applicants. The professional women, women secretaries, and women clerical workers appear similar to the hourly men on this characteristic.

Even though the government executives, bank officers, research and development managers, and teachers and administrators distribute themselves at the center and toward the low end of the scale, the positions of the 75th percentiles suggest that each of these groups contains a sizable percentage of men whose behavior is describable by this scale. The women bank tellers and women college students also show sizable percentages of this characteristic.

Exhibit 21 presents the distribution of the middle 50 percent of people in these job groups on the A_1 scale. This scale describes activity and energy levels apart from "channeled" activity. In other words, it describes free or unbounded energy. Several things are immediately apparent from this exhibit. With the exception of the two groups of salesmen and the student trainee applicants, whose scores are relatively high, the remaining groups of men show few differences between hourly and salaried employment. The groups of women show a similar mixture, with the women college students scoring high and the various job groups mixed with respect to occupational levels.

On the basis of the figures it would be difficult to predict the correlation between the A_1 and B_1 scales, both of which refer to felt energy level. The two groups of salesmen score high on both. The hourly paid men tend to be low on both. However, the research and development managers, professional women, and secretaries are low on A_1 and high on B_1. The women college students are notably high on A_1 and low on B_1. It is evident that the characteristics indicated by these two scales are differentially correlated, varying with such factors as age, development, occupational level, and the like.

Exhibit 22 shows the distributions of the middle 50 percent of scores of these 17 groups on the A_2 scale. This is the scale that describes the egocentric, introspective, self-oriented person. An examination of this exhibit shows that there are overall differences among these groups, but these differences cannot be attributed to the sex of the individuals. About the same percentage of people score low, middle, or high in any of the groups of men or women.

Many of these college students, both men and women, see themselves as having this characteristic. This may or may not be a function of their age. The hourly paid people vary across the range. Two groups of hourly

EXHIBIT 21

Middle 50 Percent of the Distributions of
Selected Job and Student Groups — A₁ Scale

Securities Salesmen

Management Trainee Applicants

Industrial Salesmen

Public School Administrators and Teachers

U.S. Government Executives

Public Utility Operators

Hourly Industrial Laborers

Bank Officers

Research and Development Managers

Hourly Workers

Women College Students

Women Bank Tellers

Women Picker Applicants

Registered Nurses

Women Clerical Workers

Professional Women

Women Secretaries

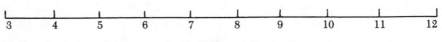

| 3 | 4 | 5 | 6 | 7 | 8 | 9 | 10 | 11 | 12 |

Scale Score — A₁

EXHIBIT 22

Middle 50 Percent of the Distributions of
Selected Job and Student Groups — A₂ Scale

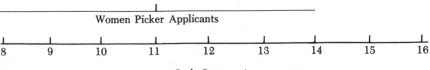

Management Trainee Applicants

Industrial Salesmen

Bank Officers

Public School Administrators and Teachers

Hourly Industrial Laborers

U.S. Government Executives

Research and Development Managers

Securities Salesmen

Public Utility Operators

Hourly Workers

Women College Students

Women Bank Tellers

Women Secretaries

Women Clerical Workers

Professional Women

Registered Nurses

Women Picker Applicants

| 8 | 9 | 10 | 11 | 12 | 13 | 14 | 15 | 16 |

Scale Score — A₂

men and the women picker applicants contain a disproportionate number of low-scoring people. By contrast, the hourly industrial laborers and women clerical workers describe themselves as having a fair amount of this characteristic.

The two groups of salesmen differ rather sharply in this characteristic, which is more marked for the industrial salesmen than for the securities salesmen.

Exhibit 23 shows the distributions of the middle 50 percent of the scores on the N_1 scale. This scale indicates the degree to which each person characterizes himself as spiritless and lacking in energy. It is evident from the exhibit that these groups score generally low on this scale. The women, with the exception of the professional women and secretaries, tend to score slightly higher than the men. The women college students score notably high — which, in conjunction with their high rank on A_1 and relatively low rank on B_1, suggests that N_1 represents a countertendency to B_1 rather than A_1.

Among the male groups, the salesmen deny this lethargic characteristic, the hourly paid industrial workers score relatively high, and the remaining groups show a similar low level.

Exhibit 24 shows the distributions of the middle 50 percent of the scores made by these groups on the N_2 scale, descriptive of the anxiety-ridden, apprehensive person.

A difference between the sexes on this characteristic is apparent here: The women exhibit this more frequently than the men. Notice, however, that the three groups of salaried women, particularly the professional women, differ relatively little from the men in general.

The two groups of salesmen, the research and development managers, and the public school administrators and teachers show little of this characteristic. It appears from these data that hourly paid people in general are more likely to be characterized by this trait.

Note that the group showing the highest median by far is the women college students. The male college students, even though scoring relatively high in contrast to the other groups of men, do not come close to the college women in this trait.

Exhibit 25 shows the distributions of the middle 50 percent of the scores of these 17 groups on the N_3 scale. This is the scale that describes the aggressive, pugnacious, and resentful individual. There is one surprise in this exhibit: the very high scores characterizing this particular sample of women college students. The men college students run high

(text continues on page 80)

EXHIBIT 23

Middle 50 Percent of the Distributions of
Selected Job and Student Groups — N_1 Scale

Hourly Industrial Workers

Bank Officers

Hourly Workers

U.S. Government Executives

Management Trainee Applicants

Public Utility Operators

R & D Managers

Public School Administrators and Teachers

Industrial Salesmen

Securities Salesmen

Women College Students

Registered Nurses

Women Bank Tellers

Women Clerical Workers

Women Picker Applicants

Women Secretaries

Professional Women

```
0     1     2     3     4     5     6     7
```

Scale Score — N_1

EXHIBIT 24

Middle 50 Percent of the Distributions of
Selected Job and Student Groups — N₂ Scale

Hourly Industrial Laborers

Hourly Workers

Management Trainee Applicants

U.S. Government Executives

Bank Officers

Public Utility Operators

Public School Administrators and Teachers

R & D Managers

Industrial Salesmen

Securities Salesmen

Women College Students

Women Clerical Workers

Women Bank Tellers

Women Picker Applicants

Women Secretaries

Registered Nurses

Professional Women

8 9 10 11 12 13 14 15 6 7 8 9 20 1 2 3 4 5 6 7 8 9 30 1 2 3 4 35

Scale Score — N₂

EXHIBIT 25

**Middle 50 Percent of the Distributions of
Selected Job and Student Groups — N₃ Scale**

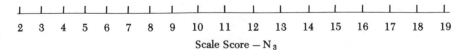

Hourly Industrial Workers

Management Trainee Applicants

Hourly Workers

Bank Officers

U.S. Government Executives

Public Utility Operators

Research and Development Managers

Public School Administrators and Teachers

Industrial Salesmen

Securities Salesmen

Women College Students

Women Picker Applicants

Women Clerical Workers

Registered Nurses

Professional Women

Women Bank Tellers

Women Secretaries

2 3 4 5 6 7 8 9 10 11 12 13 14 15 16 17 18 19

Scale Score — N₃

on this scale in comparison with other male groups, but not as high as the college women.

Two of the three groups of hourly men have relatively high scores; and, in general, both men and women hourly groups are composed of people who see themselves as responding in this way to their environment. The two groups of salesmen show as little of this characteristic, relatively speaking, as they showed on the immediately preceding measure of anxiety. We might assume from this that salesmen as a group do not respond emotionally to their environments.

SUMMARY OF DIFFERENCES BETWEEN JOB GROUPS ON THE MOTIVATION SCALES

Exhibit 26 indicates by motivation scale the job groups that are atypically high (+) or atypically low (−). The job groups are arranged in such a way as to place the groups of men at the top of the table and the groups

EXHIBIT 26
Those Job Groups Either
Atypically High (+) or Atypically Low (−) on Each Motivation Scale

Job Group	Motivation Scale										
	B_1	B_2	B_3	B_4	C_1	C_2	A_1	A_2	N_1	N_2	N_3
Securities salesmen	+	+		+	+	+	+		−	−	−
Industrial salesmen	+	+		+	+	+	+	+	−	−	−
R&D managers	+			+	−		−		−		
U.S. Government executives					−						
Public school administrators and teachers		+		+	+						−
Bank officers				+			−				
Public utility operators						−		−			
Hourly workers						−		−			
Hourly industrial laborers					−	−			+		+
Management trainee applicants		+	−		+		+	+			+
Professional women	+			+	−						
Women secretaries					−	−					
Registered nurses	−				−						
Women bank tellers							+	+		+	
Clerical workers		−		−	−					+	
Picker applicants		−		−			+	−		+	+
College students	−	−	−	−			+	+	+	+	+

of women at the bottom. Within each of these, the college student groups are placed at the bottom of the list, immediately below the men and women paid on an hourly basis.

Scanning this exhibit vertically would probably lead to the conclusion that many of these scales differentiate among job groups. This applies to most of the scales except B_3 and N_1. Three of the four B scales and the C_2 scale consistently describe these men differently from these women, and with few exceptions the men appear to have the characteristics in question more highly developed. In other words, the men describe themselves as more industrious, socially aggressive, serious minded, and assertive than do the women. Much the same can be said regarding differences between these salaried men and those paid on an hourly basis. In the case of the two A scales and the C_1 scale, the picture is confused — no consistent differences appear between men and women groups and salaried and hourly groups.

Scanning the table horizontally will reveal that certain groups are consistently atypical on these scales. The two groups of salesmen are a case in point. They are high on B_1, B_2, B_4, C_1, C_2, and A_1, and they are low on N_1, N_2, and N_3. They describe themselves as industrious, socially aggressive, serious minded, sociable, assertive, and hyperactive. They also deny being spiritless, anxiety ridden, or pugnacious. The public school administrators and teachers show a similar but less extreme pattern.

The 453 college student management trainee applicants have higher scores on B_2, C_2, A_1, A_2, and N_3 and lower scores on B_3. The women college students appear to accentuate the characteristics that distinguish women from men; they are low on the four B scales and high on the two A scales and the three N scales.

Finally, the group of professional women look much more like the salaried men than they do like the other women.

RELATIONSHIPS BETWEEN THE MOTIVATION SCALES AND THE HJSS MOTIVATION FACTORS

Chapter 4 described a technique with which it was possible to identify four collections of items in the G-ZTS related to the four HJSS motivation factor scores described in Chapter 3. These items were further sorted into 11 subsets descriptive of motivational characteristics of adults. The preceding pages have dealt with the statistical properties of measuring scales constructed from these 11 subsets of items. It would now be useful to relate the motivation *scales* to the HJSS factors, since the interpretation of some of the scales as extensions of the factors is ambiguous.

Chapter 4 pointed out that the item analyses were based on the comparison of responses made by four pairs of samples. Three of the pairs were matched samples — that is, a high HJSS A factor group of cases was compared with a low HJSS A factor group of cases, with the two groups matched or counterbalanced on the HJSS B, C, and N factors. Similar comparisons were made between high and low HJSS Factor B groups and high and low HJSS Factor C groups. The high HJSS N factor, low HJSS N factor comparison did not involve as exact a matching procedure as did that characterizing the other three.

A new set of paired samples of high-low HJSS A, B, C, and N cases was developed, following the same procedures described in Chapter 3 and using the same cutting scores on the factor continua to identify high and low cases, but matching them more exactly on the other three factors. The result was two matched A samples, each consisting of 48 cases; two matched B samples, each consisting of 54 cases; two matched C samples, each consisting of 30 cases; and two matched N samples, each consisting of 44 cases.

To determine whether the motivation scales would differentiate significantly between high and low factor groups, the differences in scale scores between high and low matched pairs were computed and the significance of the means of these differences was evaluated with the t test. This is a standard statistical procedure; t is defined as the ratio of a statistic to its standard error as estimated from the number of degrees of freedom. In this case, this t would be the ratio of the arithmetic mean of a set of differences between paired scores to the standard error of this mean difference. The magnitude of t is evaluated against a known sampling distribution to judge whether it is reasonable to assume that it occurred as a function of chance or represents a real difference between the two groups in question.

In cases where the mean difference between the groups was significant at least at the .05 level (judged to represent a real difference), the point biserial correlation coefficient was used to describe the magnitude of the correlation between the characteristic measured by the particular scale and the HJSS factor score.

This coefficient is calculated in situations where one variable is represented as a continuous series (the scale score) and the second is represented as two discrete categories or as the two extremes of a continuous series (high factor and low factor scores). It is not directly comparable to the more familiar correlation coefficient, the Pearson r. However, relative degree of correlation may be inferred by comparing one coefficient of this type with another like it.

Exhibit 27 summarizes the results of these analyses. For each of the HJSS high-low factor comparisons it shows the mean difference between the high and low groups, the value of t together with an indication of its level of significance, and the value of the point biserial correlation coefficient.

The picture that results from this set of analyses confirms what one would expect. If one examines first the data based on the high-low HJSS Factor A comparison, one observes that only the A_1 and A_2 scales differentiate significantly between these groups — one at the .05 and one at

EXHIBIT 27

**Significance of Mean Differences Between Matched High and Low
HJSS Factor Groups on the Motivation Scales Together with the
Correlation Between Individual Scales and HJSS Factors**

| | HJSS FACTORS | | | | | | | | | | | |
| | A | | | B | | | C | | | N | | |
Motivation Scale	Mean Difference	t	r Pb	Mean Difference	t	r Pb	Mean Difference	t	r Pb	Mean Difference	t	r Pb
B_1	− .48	− .52		2.28	2.49°	.24	2.67	2.10°	.19	− 2.52	− 2.33°	− .24
B_2	.17	.22		4.48	5.99‡	.45	2.07	1.59		− 1.93	− 1.89	
B_3	.56	.70		3.07	4.46‡	.38	− .33	− .33		− 2.34	− 3.19†	− .29
B_4	− .85	− 1.30		4.26	6.19‡	.53	− .43	− .52		− 2.34	− 2.86†	− .30
C_1	− .75	− .99		.61	1.01		2.17	2.89†	.26	− 1.84	− 2.89†	− .30
C_2	.48	.84		− .30	− .54		2.70	3.80‡	.35	− 1.30	− 1.77	
A_1	1.90	3.03†	.28	.00	.00		1.10	1.22		− .48	− .58	
A_2	1.40	2.02°	.19	− .20	− .25		− .20	− .20		1.32	1.53	
N_1	.65	1.48		− .65	− 1.31		− 1.20	− 1.62		2.00	3.25†	.32
N_2	.19	.14		− 2.15	− 1.45		− .10	.04		9.41	5.49‡	.53
N_3	.77	.61		− 1.30	− 1.11		− .20	.11		6.39	4.37‡	.43

°Significant at the .05 level.
†Significant at the .01 level.
‡Significant at the .001 level.

the .01 level. A_1 is apparently somewhat more highly correlated with HJSS Factor A, however, since the point biserial correlation for this relationship is higher. It is of some interest, but of no immediate significance, that the high HJSS Factor A group of cases scores higher on the B_2, B_3, C_2, N_1, N_2, and N_3 scales than does the low HJSS Factor A group and that it is lower on the B_4 and C_1 scales.

Comparisons between the high and low HJSS Factor B groups reveal that all the B scales are significantly related to this factor, as would be expected. However, B_2, B_3, and B_4 are more highly correlated with this HJSS factor than is B_1, and B_2 and B_4 appear to be most closely related. Here it is again of some interest, but of no immediate significance, that men in the high HJSS Factor B group score lower on the C_2, A_2, N_1, N_2, and N_3 scales.

The high-low HJSS C factor comparison produced a few surprises. Both C_1 and C_2 show significant relationships with the HJSS C factor, but the relationships are relatively modest in comparison to those characterizing Factor B. Surprising enough, B_1 is positively and significantly related to HJSS Factor C, and B_2 and A_1 are positively but not significantly related.

The high-low comparison for HJSS Factor N yields some unsuspected information. It is not surprising that N_1, N_2, and N_3 are positively and substantially related to the HJSS N factor. It is somewhat surprising, however, that B_1, B_3, B_4, and C_1 are negatively and significantly related to the HJSS N factor. B_2, C_2, and A_1 also show this negative relationship, but not significantly so. A_2, the egocentric scale, is the only scale other than the three N scales that appears to be positively related to the HJSS Factor N.

This analysis suggests that, in general, the two A scales should be positively correlated, the four B scales should be positively correlated, and the two C scales and B_1 should be positively correlated. All the N scales, together with A_2, should be positively correlated, and each of these four should correlate negatively with the four B scales and the two C scales. It is demonstrated later on how accurate is this prediction.

This analysis is particularly interesting in the light of the relationships that exist among the HJSS factor scores themselves. The intercorrelations among the four factors were computed on a 25 percent random sample of the 564 cases in the original HJSS sample. All these correlations were *positive* and of the following order of magnitude: $r_{AB} = +.44$; $r_{AC} = +.42$; $r_{BC} = +.46$; $r_{AN} = +.21$; $r_{BN} = +.25$; and $r_{CN} = +.28$. Despite the fact that HJSS Factors A, B, and C all correlate positively with

HJSS Factor N, the motivation scales derived from the Factor N analysis correlate *negatively* with the motivation scales derived from the Factor B and Factor C analyses and positively or negatively with those derived from the Factor A analysis. It is reasonable to assume, as was done in Chapter 2, that a reaction to sources of dissatisfaction in the environment is different from a reaction to sources of satisfaction.

INTERRELATIONSHIPS AMONG THE MOTIVATION SCALES

In the course of an analysis that is reported on later in more detail, the intercorrelations among the scales were computed for 11 of the 17 groups of men and women just discussed. A wide variety of types of people are represented in these 11 samples. They vary from high-level supervisory and management personnel to men occupying relatively low-level, hourly paid laboring jobs in industry. A number of groups of women are represented in this set of samples, including the women college students. These 11 groups of men and women varied in size from 31 to 185. The entire set comprised a total of 921 cases.

In order to get a stable measure of intercorrelation between each pair of scales, the average intercorrelation was calculated by the use of the z transformation. This mathematical transformation converts the r's which are expressed in terms of an unequal unit scale into z's which are expressed in terms of an equal unit scale. These z's can then be subjected to the usual arithmetic operations of addition and multiplication. The end product of the averaging process produces one r which is equivalent to one obtainable by treating all 921 cases as a single sample and computing the r directly. Exhibit 28 shows the complete matrix of average intercorrelations across the sample of 921 cases. In this exhibit an r of .11 would be considered significant at the .001 level.

Several sets of relationships are of interest in this exhibit. All the B scales correlate positively but not highly with one another, the highest being between B_2 and B_4. C_1 correlates positively with the four B scales and at about the same level. C_2 correlates positively with B_1 and B_2 but slightly negatively with B_3 and B_4. A_1 correlates positively with B_1, B_2, C_1, and C_2 but negatively with B_3 and B_4. A_2 does not correlate with B_1 and B_2 but correlates positively with C_2 and negatively with B_3, B_4, and C_1. N_1 and N_2 correlate negatively with all B and C scales. N_3 correlates negatively, and with some magnitude, with B_3, B_4, and C_1, positively with

EXHIBIT 28

Average Intercorrelations Among
the Motivation Scales[*]

	B_1	B_2	B_3	B_4	C_1	C_2	A_1	A_2	N_1	N_2	N_3
B_1		.19	.07	.24	.20	.30	.27	.00	− .54	− .20	− .03
B_2			.16	.34	.35	.33	.20	.08	− .29	− .29	− .08
B_3				.30	.25	− .14	− .15	− .32	− .23	− .35	− .57
B_4					.23	− .04	− .13	− .15	− .35	− .41	− .32
C_1						.25	.18	− .12	− .27	− .33	− .26
C_2							.44	.19	− .14	− .04	.19
A_1								.33	.06	.20	.25
A_2									.21	.47	.43
N_1										.51	.36
N_2											.52
N_3											

[*]Total $N = 921$.

C_2, and slightly negatively with B_1 and B_2. The three N scales and the two A scales correlate positively with each other. The two highest correlations in the table, both negative, are between B_1 and N_1 and B_3 and N_3, respectively.

Contrary to expectations, the two scales derived from the high-low HJSS Factor A comparison correlate positively with what appears to be a set of nonadaptive characteristics — those measured by the three N scales.

The consistently differential patterning of the correlations among the scales in the B, C, A, and N sets suggests that the sorting of items into subsets as described in Chapter 4 was effective in developing more homogeneous subsets. This observation is supported by the fact that equally consistent differential patterning occurs in correlations between scales across sets. As an illustration of this, A_2 correlates positively with C_2, negatively with B_3, B_4, and C_1, and essentially zero with B_1 and B_2.

This pattern of intercorrelations suggests that a relatively complex set of combinations of these measures is needed to describe people in the working population. The next chapter describes the derivation of these combinations by factor analysis procedures.

6

Factor Structure
of the Motivation Scales

THE MATERIAL PRESENTED IN CHAPTER 5, particularly that concerned with the relationships among the 11 Guilford-Zimmerman Temperament Survey motivation scales, strongly suggests that factor analyses of these scales would throw additional light on the characteristics that distinguish more highly motivated adults from those who are less highly motivated. A succession of such analyses performed on intercorrelations obtained not only from groups of salaried men but also from groups of hourly men, salaried women, hourly women, and men and women college students would either demonstrate that the descriptive system can be generalized or designate those combinations of descriptive characteristics that differentiate one type of job holder from another.

In this study a set of motivation scales was developed, using a sample of salaried working men in industry as the source of the data. The fact that such scales could be developed suggests that salaried men —whether technicians, engineers, salesmen, or managers—were at least somewhat alike in their responses to the G-ZTS. The question whether hourly men, women at either hourly or salaried levels, or college students not now working would show similar or quite different patterns can be answered by factor analysis procedures.

Most people would agree that motivation for work is a general characteristic of present or future workers and that a device descriptive of work motivation that does not describe men and women off the same basic set of dimensions is questionable. By the same line of reasoning the usefulness and validity of such a descriptive system is questionable if it cannot differentiate men and women who are more successful on industrial jobs from those who are less successful.

This chapter reports on the results of factor analyses describing patterns of relationships among the motivation scales characteristic of diverse groups of men and women. (The following chapter treats the predictive validity of the scales.)

ANALYSIS OF THE MOTIVATION SCALES IN TERMS OF OVERLAPPING ITEMS

Chapter 4 presented data showing that the 11 motivation scales overlap to some extent since the original item analyses isolated some items differentiating between high and low groups on more than one of the Hackman Job Satisfaction Schedule factor comparisons. This overlap, of course, is a function of the correlation between the A, B, C, and N HJSS factors. Since an item judged significant in two comparisons was in some cases keyed the same (that is, each keyed response was yes) and was in the other cases keyed differently (one response was yes and the other no), the correlations among the scales must in some cases be positive and in others negative.

The amount of correlation between scales to be expected from this kind of multiple scoring can be computed readily by the formula for common elements described in Chapter 3. The complete correlation matrix describing the interrelationships among the 11 motivation scales is shown in Exhibit 29. The scales in the four subsets in this exhibit are uncorrelated, as they should be. Two coefficients of some magnitude occur in the exhibit. The correlation between B_1 and N_1 is $-.31$. B_1 is of course the scale that describes the energetic, industrious person, and N_1 is the scale that describes a person with the opposite set of characteristics. The

EXHIBIT 29

**Intercorrelations Among the Motivation Scales
as a Function of Common Items**

Motivation Scales	Motivation Scales										
	B_1	B_2	B_3	B_4	C_1	C_2	A_1	A_2	N_1	N_2	N_3
B_1		.00	.00	.00	.00	.00	.00	.00	−.31	.00	.00
B_2			.00	.00	.00	.09	.00	.00	.00	.00	.00
B_3				.00	.06	−.09	.00	−.11	.00	.04	−.25
B_4					.00	−.08	.00	.00	.00	−.17	.00
C_1						.00	.00	.06	.00	.00	−.05
C_2							.00	.00	.00	−.06	.07
A_1								.00	.09	.00	.00
A_2									.00	.04	.05
N_1										.00	.00
N_2											.00
N_3											

correlation between B_3 and N_3 is −.25. B_3 describes the sympathetic, tolerant person, while N_3 describes the pugnacious, resentful person. Other correlations are of lesser magnitudes.

The R matrix presented in Exhibit 29 may be used to illustrate what the factor analysis procedure will do as a descriptive device. The R matrix was factored by the centroid solution, and the resulting factor matrix was transformed into a simpler pattern by means of orthogonal graphic rotations. Exhibit 30 shows the end product of the factor analysis. This exhibit lists the two factor patterns, together with the transformation matrix. The terminal factor pattern shows three clear-cut factors. Each of these is bimodal — that is, both positive and negative loadings on some scales occur in each. The first factor loads negatively on B_3 and positively on N_3, C_2, B_2, and A_2. The person who describes himself as pugnacious and resentful, somewhat domineering, socially aggressive, and egocentric denies that he is friendly, sympathetic, and tolerant.

The second factor loads positively on B_1 and negatively on N_1 and A_1. The person who describes himself as energetic and industrious denies that he is spiritless or hyperactive.

EXHIBIT 30

**Initial and Terminal Factor Patterns
Common Elements Analysis**

Motivation Scale	Initial Pattern			Terminal Pattern			Communality
	C_1	C_2	C_3	T_1	T_2	T_3	
B_1	− .30	.41	− .09	− .04	.51	− .08	.27
B_2	.09	.07	.06	.13	.00	.00	.02
B_3	− .38	− .29	− .20	− .52	− .01	.04	.27
B_4	.12	.09	− .35	− .02	.00	− .38	.14
C_1	− .05	− .04	− .04	− .08	.00	− .01	.01
C_2	.15	.12	.15	.24	.01	.05	.06
A_1	.09	− .11	− .10	− .04	− .14	− .09	.03
A_2	.08	.05	.09	.12	− .01	.04	.02
N_1	.34	− .49	− .01	− .02	− .60	.00	.36
N_2	− .19	− .15	.34	− .06	− .01	.41	.17
N_3	.32	.22	.19	.43	− .01	.00	.19

Transformation Matrix

	T_1	T_2	T_3
C_1	− .72	− .60	.36
C_2	− .53	.80	.27
C_3	− .45	.00	− .89

The third factor loads positively on N_2 and negatively on B_4. The person who describes himself as anxiety ridden and apprehensive denies that he is serious minded, organized, and confident.

These patterns result as a function of the correlation built into the scales. In one sense they are spurious, since they are determined mechanically. However, in a broader sense they represent a real relationship among motivational characteristics determined by the way in which men respond to the HJSS. They will appear in factor patterns derived from R matrices determined by more conventional procedures.

FACTOR ANALYSES OF DATA DERIVED FROM VARIED SAMPLES OF SUBPOPULATIONS

Chapter 5 described a set of 14 samples of men and women on the 11 motivation scales. These samples varied in size from 37 to 188 and included groups of salaried men, salaried women, hourly men, hourly women, college men, and college women. A number of the relationships among the scales and differential relationships across job groups described there suggested that factorial analyses of the R matrices constructed for each group might yield more basic information about the motivational characteristics of these men and women. Whether this would be a fruitful procedure in terms of either the ease of the factoring operation or the ultimate interpretation of the resulting factor patterns was unknown. The procedure was simply started with one group and continued until 11 had been completed. At this point it was decided to see if the 11 analyses could be summarized in some meaningful fashion. A twelfth sample was added later.

Exhibit 31 shows the groups used in this set of analyses, together with the number of cases in each. The listing is arranged so as to assemble the three groups of women in a set. Two subgroups of management trainee applicants out of a set of four are analyzed separately. Three groups of hourly paid men are listed next, followed by four groups of salaried men. Two of these salaried groups, the research and development managers, were subsequently combined and appear as one in Chapter 5.

In Appendix D are the 12 exhibits (D-1 to D-12) that show the end products of the factoring process, one for each group. In each case, the

EXHIBIT 31

**The 12 Samples of Men and Women
on Whom Factor Analyses Were Performed**

Sample	N	Type of Group
A	116	17- and 18-year-old women college students
B	114	17- and 18-year-old women mushroom-picker applicants
C	37	Women bank tellers
D	188	Production management trainee applicants
E	109	Sales management trainee applicants
F	102	Hourly paid industrial laborers
G	120	Hourly paid industrial workers
H	73	Hourly paid public utility operators
I	42	Bank officers
J	41	Research and development managers
K	44	Research and development managers
L	40	Industrial salesmen

R matrix contained product-moment correlation coefficients. An initial centroid solution was obtained, and this initial pattern was transformed into one satisfying the principles of simple structure by orthogonal graphic rotations. The exhibits are presented primarily for readers interested in the statistical procedures used, and they can be ignored conveniently by those not specifically interested in them.

Each of the 12 matrices is of rank four; that is, four factors are necessary to account for the matrix of intercorrelations. As is usual in solutions of this type, one or at most two factors are likely to account for the bulk of the variability in the R matrix. The communalities exhibit considerable variability from solution to solution, but typically those associated with the three N Scales run higher than the others. The reason for this becomes apparent later.

SIMILARITIES IN FACTOR PATTERNS

One impressive thing about the 12 sets of factor solutions is the frequency with which one of the four column vectors in a set shows up as a bimodal factor with negative factor loadings on B_2, B_3, and B_4 and positive factor loadings on N_1, N_2, and N_3. Acting on this cue, an attempt was made to locate vectors of this type in each of the factor tables. That this effort was successful is attested to by Exhibit 32. This exhibit lists by job group the vectors that appear to fit the common configuration just mentioned. The right-hand column of the exhibit gives the medians of the factor loadings for the entire set of 12 job groups on each scale. Obviously these 12 vectors have something in common: the vector defined by the set of medians. It appears to be relatively invariant across the 12 samples.

The vector is defined by high positive loadings on N_2 and N_3 and moderately high positive loadings on A_2, N_1, and A_1. Negative loadings of some magnitude occur in association with B_3 and B_4 and lower negative loadings occur on C_1 and B_2. The pattern then characterizes a person who describes himself as anxiety ridden and apprehensive (N_2), pugnacious and resentful (N_3), egocentric (A_2), spiritless (N_1), and hyperactive (A_1). Such a person denies that he is tolerant and sympathetic (B_3), serious minded and confident (B_4), sociable and respectful (C_1), and socially aggressive and competitive (B_2). This combination of traits seems to characterize

EXHIBIT 32

"Anxiety" Vectors Together with Measures of Closeness of Fit to the "Median" Vector

Motivation Scale	A	B	C	D	E	F	G	H	I	J	K	L	Median Loading
						Job Groups							
N_2	.47	.74	.86	.63	.78	.60	.65	.75	.86	.79	.72	.64	.73
N_3	.70	.79	.84	.45	.73	.66	.80	.80	.51	.74	.69	.76	.73
A_2	.33	.67	.43	.46	.69	.26	.38	.66	.74	.50	.71	.56	.53
N_1	.33	.50	.60	.25	.34	.51	.36	.44	.42	.47	.57	.44	.44
A_1	.05	.62	.48	.08	.28	.32	.23	.38	.29	.13	.38	.33	.30
C_2	.21	.26	− .03	.00	.12	.19	− .04	.28	.05	.24	.26	.02	.15
B_3	− .58	− .51	− .57	− .57	− .64	− .72	− .76	− .63	− .21	− .60	− .19	− .52	− .51
B_4	− .48	− .38	− .61	− .35	− .34	− .42	− .63	− .57	− .25	− .47	− .26	− .53	− .47
C_1	− .31	− .23	− .45	− .48	− .55	− .41	− .40	− .30	− .32	− .48	− .05	− .25	− .36
B_2	− .15	− .13	− .46	− .57	− .27	− .38	− .47	− .11	− .06	.09	.04	− .08	− .14
B_1	− .07	− .02	− .11	.06	.03	− .14	− .06	− .02	− .08	− .14	− .30	− .10	− .07

Factor						*D Values*							
Anxiety	.19	.17	.26	.43	.14	.21	.28	.08	.27	.12	.40	.05	.00
Aggression	.69	1.81	2.21	1.16	1.64	1.23	1.47	1.69	1.60	1.97	1.65	1.23	1.33
Achievement	1.90	2.46	3.65	2.39	2.58	2.73	3.26	2.67	1.61	2.40	1.66	2.15	2.22
Status	2.99	3.27	4.90	3.86	4.11	3.66	4.53	3.68	3.12	3.75	2.69	3.31	3.92
Drive	4.02	5.00	6.52	4.39	5.10	5.04	5.59	5.23	4.52	5.18	4.83	4.81	4.82

a person who is responding emotionally and negatively to people and social situations, rather than cognitively and positively. This combination might be labeled an "anxiety" factor and would be judged basically nonadaptive as far as successful work in industry is concerned.

At the bottom of Exhibit 32 are sets of values that reflect the degree of similarity between the vector characterizing any one group and the median of all the groups. The row labeled "anxiety" gives the values comparing these individual vectors with the median pattern just described. This statistic (D) is obtained by finding the sum of the squared differences between the elements of any job group vector and the corresponding elements of the median vector, or, for example,

$$D = .19 = \Sigma[(.47 - .73)^2; (.70 - .73)^2; \ldots (- .07 - -.07)^2]$$

The magnitude of these D values reflects the degree of similarity between any given group vector and the median vector.

The interpretation of this statistic is made obvious if we show along with the D value for the anxiety pattern the corresponding values of D when each job group vector is compared with the other "median" vectors that appear consistently in the 12 factor patterns. Note that these other D's are sizably larger, indicating a much better fit to the anxiety pattern than to any other. It would appear, however, that the particular pattern we are identifying as an anxiety factor is related more closely to the aggression factor than to the other three, since the D values computed against this median vector are smaller.

A second examination of the terminal factors in the 12 samples identified a pattern that seemed to be characterized by high positive loadings on B_1 and high negative loadings on N_1. Twelve such vectors were located, one from each of the samples, as shown in Exhibit 33. In this exhibit the motivation scales have again been rearranged so that the definitive scales of the vector appear together at the top of the exhibit. In all samples,

EXHIBIT 33

"Drive" Vectors Together with Measures of Closeness of Fit to the "Median" Vector

Motivation Scale	A	B	C	D	E	F	G	H	I	J	K	L	Median Loading
B_1	.65	.70	.75	.57	.69	.65	.58	.69	.76	.72	.63	.76	.69
C_2	.37	.63	.48	.00	− .06	.56	.09	.41	.35	.61	.24	.66	.39
A_1	.04	.31	.41	− .01	− .02	.37	− .10	.17	.28	.41	.47	.29	.28
B_2	.14	.58	.37	.28	.05	.38	.14	− .03	.16	.28	.42	.50	.28
B_4	.16	.34	.33	.57	.42	.09	.35	− .12	.05	.07	.40	.07	.24
N_1	− .75	− .52	− .61	− .79	− .76	− .54	− .58	− .71	− .82	− .64	− .34	− .76	− .67
N_2	− .43	− .40	− .06	− .40	− .02	− .48	− .22	− .12	− .11	− .29	− .24	− .32	− .26
B_3	− .03	.25	.09	.07	.19	− .01	.01	− .27	.09	− .38	.08	− .29	.04
C_1	.01	.47	.29	.15	− .02	.12	.23	.03	.09	.09	.00	.13	.10
A_2	− .12	.03	.05	.01	.00	− .11	− .02	− .01	.15	.02	.07	.09	.01
N_3	.00	− .06	.22	− .19	− .08	− .04	.15	.11	− .20	.07	.04	.20	.02

Factors							D Values						
Drive	.15	.39	.17	.44	.49	.16	.32	.37	.17	.28	.23	.32	.00
Status	1.65	.97	.99	2.01	2.19	.97	1.51	1.56	1.47	1.20	.89	1.42	1.14
Achievement	1.93	1.95	1.52	1.79	1.61	1.92	1.19	1.92	1.89	2.05	1.09	2.13	1.55
Aggression	2.05	3.21	2.38	2.61	2.31	2.30	1.55	1.54	2.51	2.01	2.07	2.38	2.12
Anxiety	5.19	6.34	4.70	6.29	5.10	5.18	4.54	3.73	4.95	4.94	4.31	4.96	4.82

B_1 has a large positive loading and N_1 has a large negative loading. The other scales in the pattern do not show the same degree of consistency. The measures of pattern similarity, the D values at the bottom of the table, again indicate that a vector in the set is much more like the median vector of this set than it is like any other median vector.

This pattern is characteristic of a person who describes himself as energetic and industrious (B_1), authoritative and assertive (C_2), hyperactive (A_1), socially aggressive (B_2), and serious minded and confident (B_4). The same person would deny that he is spiritless or lacking in energy (N_1) or anxiety ridden and apprehensive (N_2). The outstanding feature of this vector is the very high loadings on B_1 and N_1. A person with this vector might well be described as one with a high level of directed energy or sheer drive, and it is labeled a *drive* factor.

At this point in the analysis exactly one-half the factor patterns had been accounted for. Two vectors from each sample could be assigned to one or the other of the preceding general factors. The same search technique was tried on the remaining 24 vectors. An interesting combination of B_2, C_1, C_2, and A_1 appeared in the remaining set of vectors. Isolating these produced the combination shown in Exhibit 34. This vector appears in 11 of the 12 samples. As indicated, it seems to be characterized by high positive loadings on B_2, C_1, C_2, and A_1 and on nothing else with any degree of consistency. An occasional job-group vector exhibits slight departures from this pattern, but the central core is there. This pattern is unrelated to the three N scales; it is unimodal in contrast to the preceding two.

This vector is characteristic of a person who describes himself as authoritative and assertive (C_2), hyperactive (A_1), sociable and deferent (C_1), and socially aggressive (B_2). It describes a person adept at playing a variety of social roles, alternating a dominant (C_2) or deferent (C_1) role to suit the situation. This pattern comes close to describing the stereotype of the status seeker or prestige seeker. It might be called a *status* factor.

Again, the individual job sample vectors are much more like the median vector of this set than like the median vectors of any other set (see the D values at the bottom of the exhibit).

Now 13 vectors remained that did not fit any one of the three general factors just described. Did these also exhibit an order that makes sense? Exhibit 35 shows what happened when six vectors coming from each of six different samples were isolated as a set. These appear to be characterized in their entirety by high positive loadings on N_3 and high negative loadings on B_3. Individual job-group vectors have other variables (scales) attached to these two.

EXHIBIT 34

"Status" Vectors Together with Measures of Closeness
of Fit to the "Median" Vector

Motivation Scale	A	C	D	E	F	G	H	I	J	K	L	Median Loading
					Job Groups							
A_1	.57	.32	.60	.69	.52	.71	.59	.50	.46	.23	.67	.57
C_2	.58	.48	.51	.60	.52	.68	.39	.81	.41	.73	.54	.54
C_1	.57	.47	.48	.24	.58	.49	.47	.63	.65	.66	.13	.49
B_2	.35	.49	.03	.06	.23	.42	.62	.81	.54	.45	.32	.42
B_1	.34	− .07	.54	.11	.11	.35	.11	.00	.02	.13	.28	.11
B_3	− .11	.07	.05	.00	.02	− .05	.03	.13	− .07	− .42	.07	.02
B_4	− .04	.09	− .05	− .43	.05	.07	.04	.22	− .10	.03	.09	.04
A_2	.10	.12	.00	− .02	.06	.25	.36	.01	.30	.08	.54	.10
N_1	− .16	.00	− .09	.01	.07	− .01	− .06	− .01	.01	− .45	− .08	− .01
N_2	− .05	− .07	− .02	.06	.07	− .13	− .18	− .25	− .04	− .43	− .13	− .07
N_3	− .02	− .28	.15	.05	− .06	.12	.00	− .08	− .22	.03	− .28	-- .02
Factor					*D Values*							
Status	.11	.18	.40	.47	.08	.15	.15	.35	.19	.70	.45	.00
Achievement	1.32	.90	1.47	1.67	1.05	1.32	.89	1.71	1.10	1.92	1.11	1.01
Drive	.88	1.38	.84	1.63	1.35	1.11	1.23	1.72	1.63	1.11	1.10	1.14
Aggression	1.76	1.76	1.71	1.53	1.60	2.02	1.84	2.92	1.79	1.94	2.16	1.67
Anxiety	3.59	3.87	3.28	2.45	3.21	3.56	3.63	5.34	3.65	4.86	3.54	3.42

The pattern is characteristic of a person who describes himself as aggressive, pugnacious, and resentful (N_3) and denies that he is sympathetic, friendly, and tolerant (B_3). It distinguishes the person who is irritated by almost anything that goes on around him, is particularly bothered by people, and reacts to irritation with overt, aggressive acts. This might be called an *aggression* factor.

Finally, seven vectors remained. Arranged as a set they appear as Exhibit 36. These seven vectors also appear to have something in common, and the pattern that characterizes them is represented by A_2, B_2, and B_4. There is a suggestion here that both N_2 and N_3 may be components of the pattern, but these scales are not represented as consistently as are the other three. Interestingly, their loadings are positive, suggesting that a certain amount of emotionality accompanies the basic pattern.

EXHIBIT 35

"Aggression" Vectors Together with Measures of Closeness
of Fit to the "Median" Vector

Motivation Scale	B	C	Job Groups D	H	I	K	Median Loading
N_3	.31	.29	.59	.32	.75	.55	.43
B_3	− .54	− .43	− .52	− .28	− .68	− .57	− .53
B_1	− .02	.04	− .15	.18	− .03	− .03	− .03
B_2	− .03	.04	.46	.13	− .11	− .13	.00
B_4	.07	− .20	− .06	.34	− .21	− .31	− .13
C_1	− .42	− .01	.07	− .03	.09	− .43	− .02
C_2	− .10	.07	.42	− .03	− .03	.05	.01
A_1	− .22	− .03	.30	− .09	− .28	− .02	− .05
A_2	− .01	.45	.37	.21	.02	− .07	.11
N_1	.11	.06	.09	− .21	.06	.05	.07
N_2	− .04	.03	.16	− .12	.01	− .01	.00
Factor			*D Values*				
Aggression	.27	.16	.65	.46	.22	.27	.00
Achievement	1.20	.66	.83	.48	1.68	1.72	.91
Anxiety	1.81	1.20	1.28	2.55	1.59	1.24	1.33
Status	2.53	1.47	1.14	1.47	2.67	2.59	1.67
Drive	2.47	1.99	2.34	1.09	3.02	2.72	2.12

This pattern characterizes men and women who describe themselves as egocentric (A_2), socially aggressive and competitive (B_2), and serious minded and confident (B_4). The rather peculiar make-up of this factor, in particular the association of egocentricity with objective social attitudes and work style, suggests that the pattern may be descriptive of an achievement-oriented person, and this might be called an *achievement* factor. It comes as close as any other combination of scales to what was called accomplishment motivation in the HJSS analysis, and it represents the kind of fusion of social and accomplishment motivation described by one of the HJSS factors seen in the supervisory and managerial group.

An analysis of the *D* values at the bottom of Exhibit 36 suggests that this general factor is more like the status and aggression factors than the drive and anxiety factors.

The five general factors defined by the median loadings have been assembled in Exhibit 37. In this exhibit the five factors are arranged so as to place the three that appear to be adaptive patterns to the left, with the two nonadaptive patterns on the right. The loadings that define the

EXHIBIT 36

"Achievement" Vectors Together with
Measures of Goodness of Fit to the
"Median" Vector

Motivation Scale	Job Groups							Median Loading
	A	B	E	F	G	J	L	
A_2	.57	.45	.05	.62	.46	.32	.01	.45
B_2	.42	.43	.53	.42	.37	.53	.27	.42
B_4	.12	.25	.36	.29	.21	.48	.47	.29
B_1	.25	− .02	.06	.08	− .01	.05	− .27	.05
B_3	.10	.06	.00	.08	.06	− .10	− .07	.06
C_1	.06	.12	.01	.06	.02	.08	− .40	.06
C_2	.09	.06	.24	.12	.27	− .15	.06	.09
A_1	.40	− .03	.01	.37	.15	− .07	− .07	.01
N_1	.06	.13	− .14	.20	.22	− .19	− .01	.06
N_2	.42	.17	− .29	.25	.33	− .03	− .17	.17
N_3	.22	.08	.31	.50	.27	− .11	.06	.22
Factor			*D Values*					
Achievement	.30	.04	.47	.27	.12	.37	.73	.00
Aggression	1.36	.97	1.01	1.28	.99	1.28	1.03	.91
Status	.97	1.00	.93	1.16	.94	1.37	1.82	1.01
Drive	1.69	1.75	.95	2.10	1.94	1.36	1.91	1.55
Anxiety	1.83	2.36	3.44	1.79	1.66	3.68	3.16	2.22

EXHIBIT 37

Derived Factor Pattern
Median Loadings

Motivation Scale	Drive	Status	General Factor Achievement	Anxiety	Aggression
B_1	.69*	.11	.05	− .07	− .03
B_2	.28*	.42*	.42*	− .14	.00
B_3	.04	.02	.06	− .51*	− .53*
B_4	.24*	.04	.29*	− .47*	− .13
C_1	.10	.49*	.06	− .36*	− .02
C_2	.39*	.54*	.09	.15	.01
A_1	.28*	.57*	.01	.30*	− .05
A_2	.01	.10	.45*	.53*	.11
N_1	− .67*	− .01	.06	.44*	.07
N_2	− .26*	− .07	.17*	.73*	.00
N_3	.02	− .02	.22*	.73*	.43*

*Elements characterizing the patterns.

factors are specified with an asterisk. The five columns represent the drive factor, the status or prestige factor, the achievement factor, the anxiety factor, and the aggression factor.

B_1, the scale that describes how energetically and industriously a person works, occurs in only one of these factors. All the other scales occur in at least two, with B_2, B_4, and A_1 occurring in three. The drive factor is defined by seven scales; the status factor, by four; the achievement factor, by five; the anxiety factor, by eight; and the aggression factor, by two.

FACTOR ANALYSIS OF THE MATRIX OF AVERAGE r's

Exhibit 28 in the preceding chapter shows the set of average intercorrelations among the scales across 11 of the 12 samples used in the preceding analysis. (Sample F had not been factor analyzed at the time the average r's were computed.) PSP thought it would be informative to factor analyze this matrix in order to see whether the pattern shown in Exhibit 37 could be partially or completely duplicated. Exhibit D-13 in Appendix D shows the initial and terminal factor patterns emerging from this analysis. In this case, as in the preceding 12, a centroid solution was used and the centroid pattern was rotated to simple structure by means of orthogonal graphic rotations.

Five centroid factors were extracted, and when they were transformed into a psychologically meaningful pattern a *near duplication of the matrix shown in Exhibit 37* resulted. Not only did the same five factors reappear, but the magnitudes of the factor loadings were exceedingly close in the two solutions. How close they were is attested by the product-moment correlations across the "median" and "average r" solutions. One of these correlations is .89 for the achievement comparison; the others vary between .95 and .99, indicating very close relationships between the two sets of factors.

An examination of Exhibit 37 or the terminal pattern of the average r solution shown in Exhibit D-13 suggests that a set of oblique rotations might simplify the pattern. An oblique rotation, according to factor analytic methods, eliminates the correlation between any two factors and leaves as a residual pattern those variables that are uniquely correlated with each one.

The end product of such an analysis performed on the average r solution is shown in Exhibit D-14 in Appendix D. The analysis demonstrates a sizable positive correlation between V_1 and V_4, as well as between V_2 and V_3. Translating this into the labels used to identify the factors, the anxiety and aggression factors are positively correlated, as one would anticipate; and the status and drive factors are also positively correlated.

What is left after such an analysis is a collection of relatively "pure" factors, reflecting their essential elements. These are shown in Exhibit 38. In this exhibit the factor loadings that characterize the factors have been boxed. The drive factor consists now of B_1, B_4, and N_1. It characterizes a person who describes himself as very energetic and industrious; tends to describe himself as serious minded, organized, and confident; and strongly denies that he is lacking in energy. The three scales together are describing a work-oriented directed-drive characteristic. Notice that the loading on A_1, the scale describing a person with free-floating, nondirected energy, drops out of the pattern.

EXHIBIT 38

Oblique Factor Pattern
Combined Samples

Motivation Scale	Drive	Status	Achievement	Anxiety	Aggression	Scale Description
B_1	.64	.07	− .04	− .09	− .08	Industriousness
B_2	− .02	.47	.43	− .11	− .05	Social aggressiveness
B_3	.02	− .01	− .02	− .05	− .50	Social tolerance
B_4	.17	.00	.39	− .32	− .09	Serious mindedness
C_1	− .05	.46	.07	− .11	− .16	Sociability
C_2	.04	.58	.00	.05	.11	Assertiveness
A_1	.04	.53	− .01	.36	− .10	Hyperactivity
A_2	.07	.13	.34	.48	− .03	Egocentricity
N_1	− .58	.04	− .04	.38	.07	Spiritlessness
N_2	− .03	− .12	.03	.63	− .07	Apprehensiveness (anxiety)
N_3	− .05	.10	.13	.20	.44	Aggression

Oblique Pattern

Note: The variables that define the factors are boxed.

The other vector markedly affected by this transformation is the anxiety factor. The two most dramatic changes involve B_3 and N_3. B_3 shifts from $-.52$ to $-.05$ and N_3 from $.65$ to $.20$. These two scales, of course, specify the aggression factor. The other three that drop out of this pattern are B_2 ($-.21$ to $-.11$), C_1 ($-.31$ to $-.11$), and C_2 ($.18$ to $.05$). The anxiety factor in pure form characterizes the person who describes himself as anxiety ridden and apprehensive (N_2), egocentric (A_2), spiritless (N_1), and hyperactive (A_1) and who denies that he is serious minded, organized, and confident (B_4).

INTERPRETATION OF THE FACTORS

The analyses just decribed are significant for at least two reasons. The first reason is tied to the similarities and differences that exist between these factors and those derived from the analyses of Herzberg's data (Chapter 2) and the HJSS items used in attitude surveys. The second reason is concerned with the way in which the system describes not only salaried men working in industry but also hourly men, hourly and salaried women, and young men and women about to enter the job market. From a theoretical point of view the second reason is of more significance, since it suggests that motivation as described by this system is a common characteristic of employable adults, and the factors are the parameters of a work motivation system.

If the first reason is considered for a moment, a discussion of the factors can be made meaningful by retracing the steps involved in their generation. As indicated earlier, the reanalysis of Herzberg's interview data led to the rather startling conclusion that words descriptive of *feeling* states could signify the way motivation was *channeled* and the developmental level reached by a person, motivationally speaking. Two distinct channels could be identified: one channel appeared to characterize a man who could be described as a *closure seeker*, and the level at which he operated could be determined by whether he needed support from others for this experience, was partially emancipated from this support, or was entirely emancipated from it. Social stimuli play a minor role in this type of *accomplishment* motivation. Reinforcing agents on the job were interesting and challenging work, successful completion of a job, permissive supervision, and praise for work accomplished. A second channel was *social stimulation*. Here people reported feelings of status, responsibility, and personal growth, accompanying satisfaction derived from being given supervisory responsibility over others, good work by subordinates, and being given a promotion.

Two other feeling states were reported: financial well-being and growth, and security. Both these feelings appeared to have something in common with the two channels just described, but apparently they were generated by a mixture of the job conditions that produced the accomplishment and social stimulation patterns. Where accomplishment appeared to be *task*-oriented and social stimulation appeared to be *situation*-oriented — but *both* were job-oriented — financial growth and security as feelings appeared to reflect a type of reinforcement coming from events and conditions extrinsic to the job itself.

A questionnaire variant of Herzberg's interview was included as part of an attitude survey. Analyses of the feelings accompanying satisfaction on the job and of job conditions producing that satisfaction isolated three factors or channels. Two of these were the task-oriented and situation-oriented channels. A third, which was called a "money-status" orientation, was distinct, but overlapped the first two channels to some extent. All three channels were positively correlated, one with the other, indicating that motivation channeling occurs in combinations or patterns in working adults.

In the Herzberg interview data no clear-cut patterns of relationships were found between sources of dissatisfaction on the job and feelings accompanying them. These feelings, although in part expressions of the absence of positive feelings, tended to be emotional in tone, reflecting states such as anger, disgust, anxiety, fear, and the like. Analyses performed on the survey data asking about periods of dissatisfaction did not yield clear-cut patterns of relationships. The relationships existed, but apparently they varied so much from person to person that no generalizable pattern could be discerned.

When the three positive factor patterns — accomplishment, social stimulation, and money-status — were related to items on the G-ZTS, eight collections of items were isolated, the responses to which correlated with the responses to the three HJSS factor patterns. Four of these collections were associated with the social-stimulation factor and two each with the accomplishment and money-status factors.

In this analysis high and low A, B, or C factor men were being contrasted when the effect of the other factors had been removed; that is, without the compensating influence of the other factors. This is comparable to asking what a person is like who is motivated only by accomplishment (or any other single factor) in contrast to one who has none of this motivation. Some surprising descriptions resulted from these analyses. The high accomplishment people (HJSS Factor A) describe themselves on the G-ZTS as egocentric or hyperactive, with their hyperactivity being of a nonwork directed type. Their energies are directed toward satisfying their own personal desires without concern for socially determined goals or external social pressures. In extreme form such persons might be described as perfectionistic — closure-seeking in the most extreme form.

The high money-status people (HJSS Factor C) describe themselves as deferent, respectful, sociable people on the one hand or as assertive, authoritative, domineering people on the other. These two descriptions do not appear, on first glance, to be compatible. However, they characterize people adept at two types of social role playing, both required in many occupational hierarchies. Generally speaking, a manager has both superiors and subordinates. The ability to play both roles is a must for anyone aspiring to climb either the occupational or social ladder.

This is an apt characterization of status-oriented people. Perhaps such people should be described not only as status seeking, but also as prestige seeking—the two terms presupposing somewhat different types of value systems.

The high social-stimulation people (HJSS Factor B) think of themselves in terms of four collections of items. They are tolerant, friendly, and sympathetic (B_3) or serious-minded, organized, ambitious, and confident (B_4) or socially aggressive, dynamic, and competitive (B_2) or energetic, industrious, and vigorous (B_1). B_3 and B_4 describe characteristic ways of responding to the pressures of a social milieu with B_4 representing a work style in an organized work system. B_3 describes the social-stimulation seeker in pure form — a person who enjoys people, singly or in groups. In extreme form B_3 describes the sociable person who gets nothing done himself and interferes with others who are trying to get their work done. The collection B_4 describes the hard-working, dedicated 24-hour-a-day man who is probably without a sense of humor, has little time for his family, and talks only shop in a social situation.

The collection B_2 describes the born leader: dynamic, highly competitive, admired, and respected, but probably not well liked. As for B_1, it describes how much energy can be mustered routinely to accomplish one's goals and those of society.

The N, or negative, factor on the HJSS simply reflects how many things a person can be irritated by or made unhappy by on the job. A high-scoring person would be easily irritated; in contrast, a low-scoring person presumably can take things in stride. Three collections of items broke out of the item analysis done on the G-ZTS. One describes a lethargic person — one who is spiritless and lacking in energy (N_1). A second collection describes an anxiety-ridden, apprehensive person (N_2), and a third describes a pugnacious, resentful, aggressive person (N_3). The latter two collections represent the two general ways of responding to emotional stimuli — with fear or anger or with anxiety or aggression. These collections make sense against our original assumptions about reports of unhappy episodes — that they represent emotional responses to job situations and events and are a class of experience different from those reported in connection with happy episodes.

Eight of the 11 scales directly reflect ways in which motivation is channeled and the temperamental characteristics of those men and women whose motivation is channeled differentially. More of them are situation-oriented or people-oriented than are task-oriented or self-oriented. However, this simply may be a function of the kinds of items found in the G-ZTS.

Of peculiar interest is the appearance of three descriptions of the amount of energy characterizing a person. Two of the three descriptions are of both amount and direction, or channeling; the third denies its presence. The B_1 scale exemplifies the energetic, vigorous, *industrious* person. The A_1 scale describes the hyperactive person with free-floating energy. Both scales show the presence of high-energy levels: One describes directed energy; the other denies it. Two of these scales, B_1 and N_1, combined with B_4 (the work-style scale) define a *drive* factor. The A_1 scale appears in a *status* factor as a positive characteristic and also in an *anxiety* factor as a negative characteristic. The energy characteristic, of course, did not appear in Herzberg's data or in the data based on HJSS items.

The general factor identified as achievement (B_2, B_4, and A_2) represents a socially modified form of the accomplishment factor described in the survey material. This could just as well be termed a closure factor if it is assumed that successful completion of a job (closure) is the primary reinforcing agent. A_2 by itself appears to describe closure seeking; A_2 plus B_4 may well exemplify accomplishment seeking; and A_2, B_4, and B_2, all maximized, may characterize achievement seeking.

What we have called the status or prestige factor (B_2, C_1, C_2, and A_1) is a curious mixture of the three positive HJSS factors. It contains the undirected or non-work-oriented drive characteristic (A_1), the two role-playing scales (C_1 and C_2), and the social-aggressiveness scale (B_2). This combination makes sense if it is remembered that the feeling of status was an element in the social-stimulation factor derived from an analysis of Herzberg's data. It also was a component of the HJSS B factor in some analyses performed on the survey data. Apparently, to be the kind of person described by B_2, C_1, and C_2 it is necessary to have a fair amount of free-floating energy.

The two nonadaptive patterns, anxiety and aggression, contain the N scales positively weighted and two of the B scales negatively weighted. Anxiety and aggression, then, are people-tied, and this jibes with the original assumptions about the pervasiveness of social stimuli in producing emotional responses.

The original assumptions about the relative importance of accomplishment (HJSS Factor A) and social-stimulation (HJSS Factor B) motivation do not appear to be supported by this factor structure. Accomplishment motivation in pure form is highly egocentric and apparently somewhat nonadaptive as far as working in industry is concerned. HJSS Factor B motivation, on the other hand, is reflected in all five of the motivation factors and always in an adaptive form. It is also the motivation that isolated the directed energy factor, which has been labeled the drive factor.

The significance of the distributed nature of the motivation factors cannot be overestimated. This system can be criticized on the grounds that it is based solely on the kinds of items contained in the Guilford-Zimmerman Temperament Survey. It is conceivable that other kinds of instruments of this same general type, whether purporting to measure personality characteristics, temperament characteristics, interests, or values, would expand the system described here. It would be surprising if they did not. The real importance to be attached to these data is simply that this descriptive system, whether basically or superficially descriptive of motivated people, nevertheless characterizes not only salaried men but also salaried women, hourly men and women, and young men and women college students. The consistency of these data argues strongly for the construct validity of the whole system.

On numerous occasions this book has alluded to the adaptive or nonadaptive nature of certain of the motivation scales or motivation factors derived from them. These allusions presuppose that the scales not only have what is commonly called construct validity but have predictive validity as well. Chapter 7 shows just how useful these scales and factors are in the prediction of criteria of success in industrial jobs.

Predictive Validities
of the Motivation Scales
and the Motivation Factors

IN THE COURSE of its work with industry, Psychological Service of Pittsburgh often constructs selection systems and validates them against a variety of types of work-performance criteria. In some cases these systems are set up, permitted to collect data, and then validated after performance criteria become available. In other cases an intact work group is examined, ratings or other estimates of work performance are obtained, and the relationships between selection criteria (personal history items, tests, questionnaires, interviews) and performance criteria are determined. Selection standards specified for use on the basis of this kind of analysis are reevaluated (crossvalidated) at later periods.

The criteria with which PSP usually works are simple and not particularly sensitive, but they are uniformly meaningful for the particular company or job. Generally they serve to assign employees to two or at most four groups. Into one group go individuals who are clearly outstanding performers. Into a second group go individuals who are clearly substandard — those whose performance does not meet the requirements of the work system of which they are a part. Into a third or a fourth group go those who are judged to be good or acceptable — or, more typically, they are assigned to an intermediate "acceptable" group.

Statistical tests performed on data categorized in this fashion generally show that the substandard or poor group can be differentiated from the other two on the basis of a variety of measures. However, only infrequently does PSP find that a selection variable or collection thereof will distinguish an outstanding group from the other two. Selection systems tend to be elimination systems; they identify people who are unlikely candidates for a job. As positive prediction systems, they leave something to be desired.

Not only should motivation measures as predictors of success on the job function as positive predictors, but, in contrast to measures of other human characteristics, they should be generally applicable to any job — at least certain aspects of motivation should be. For example, it seemed predictable that the drive factor would be correlated with job performance in most kinds of situations, that the anxiety factor would correlate negatively with performance criteria in all kinds of industrial jobs, and that the aggression factor would correlate negatively with performance criteria in most kinds of industrial jobs. This chapter will show how accurate these predictions proved to be.

PREDICTIVE VALIDITIES OF THE 11 MOTIVATION SCALES

What follows offers evidence on the predictive validities of the 11 motivation scales for a variety of jobs in industry; presents evidence on the predictive validities of the five motivation factors described in the preceding chapter; and describes the range of individual differences in these five motivation factors for a variety of groups of working men and women.

Exhibit 39 summarizes the relationships between each of the 11 motivation scales and performance criteria obtained for seven quite different types of jobs. Sample A consists of 42 hourly production and maintenance workers assigned to one of two groups: a high group of 19 men and a low group of 23 men. The criterion was based on the relative rate of progress in production supervision over an eight-year span. Those in the high group made outstanding progress; those in the low group made minimal progress or none at all. These 42 men were hourly paid production or maintenance workers at the time they responded to the items on the Guilford-Zimmerman Temperament Survey.

Sample B consists of 73 men in a public utility occupying either control-room operator jobs or lower-level jobs in that progression. The criterion was based on a set of ratings from two independent judges relative to work performance and attitude toward the job. These 73 men were split into one group of 18 men judged to be excellent performers and a second combined group of 19 men judged good, 18 judged satisfactory, and 18 judged poor.

Sample C consists of 29 women bank tellers of whom 9 were judged to be excellent; the remaining 20, acceptable or poor. The criterion was developed from ratings made by supervisors on a multiscale rating system, one component of which was ability to sell.

Sample D consists of 27 technical managers rated for their technical ability and managerial potential by their two immediate supervisors. Of the 27, 9 were clearly assignable to an outstanding group; the remaining 18 were judged to be good, acceptable, or poor.

Sample E consists of 31 technical salesmen rated for their sales ability and managerial potential by their two immediate supervisors. Seven of these men clearly were assignable to an outstanding group on both rating criteria; the remaining 24 were classifiable as possessing lesser degrees of these two characteristics.

Sample F consists of 49 industrial salesmen. These men were referred to PSP for the purpose of setting standards for the selection of future employees. Of these men 20 were judged to be clearly outstanding. The remaining 29 were men either being discharged or judged to be questionable risks.

G is a sample of 36 securities salesmen seen by PSP as appraisal cases, either for selection or for general evaluation. Subsequently, their performance was evaluated by two of their immediate supervisors. Of these, 11 could be clearly assigned to an outstanding category; the remaining 25 were rated either satisfactory or poor.

These criterion groups were constituted in this way. For Samples A and F no meaningful intermediate group was available; consequently, evidence of validity had to be obtained by a comparison of two extreme groups. In these cases the measure of correlation used to evaluate the magnitude of the relationships between individual motivation scales and the performance criterion was the point biserial correlation coefficient (measure of relationship between a continuous variable and a real dichotomy).

In the remaining samples, the distributions of scale scores strongly suggested that differentiation between low, intermediate, and high criterion groups occurred only when the low and intermediate groups were combined and contrasted with the high group. In these samples the magnitude of the correlation between a given scale and the criterion was determined by the biserial correlation coefficient (measure of relationship between a continuous variable and an arbitrarily dichotomized continuous one).

In Exhibit 39 the point biserial or biserial coefficient, as appropriate, is listed for each scale for each high-low criterion group comparison.

EXHIBIT 39

Motivation Scale Validities

	A	B	C	D	E	F	G
	Hourly Production Workers	Public Utility Operators	Women Bank Tellers	Technical Managers	Technical Salesmen	Industrial Salesmen	Securities Salesmen
B₁	.03	.16	.18	.55°	.17	.37°	.45°
B₂	.24	− .05	.24	.58°	.15	− .02	.16
B₃	.34°	.15	.71°	.22	− .11	− .16	− .02
B₄	.13	.43°	.57°	.31	.10	.36°	− .07
C₁	.23	.22	.35	.55°	− .07	− .13	. 02
C₂	.09	− .06	.18	.83°	.40	.28°	. 11
A₁	.11	− .15	− .35	.14	− .01	.10	.02
A₂	− .16	− .25	− .30	− .02	.30	.15	− .13
N₁	− .29	− .13	− .51	− .39	.14	− .30°	− .40°
N₂	− .31°	− .18	− .64°	− .65°	− .11	− .31°	− .23
N₃	− .25	− .24	− .71°	− .34	− .04	− .34°	− .09

°An asterisk accompanying a coefficient indicates statistically significant differentiation between the two criterion groups at least at the .05 level of significance. These coefficients are biserial correlations, with the exception of those in A and F, which are point biserial coefficients.

Along with these are indications of the statistical significance of the differences between the means of the high and low groups as determined by the t test. The .05 level was arbitrarily chosen as the critical level of significance.

Scanning this table vertically reveals that work performance can be predicted from these scales most efficiently for Sample C, the women bank tellers; Sample D, the technical managers; and Sample F, which is the group of industrial salesmen. The number of scales showing statistically significant relationships with the criterion are four in the case of Sample C, five in Sample D, and six in Sample F.

When the table is scanned horizontally, evidences of validity emerge. All the correlations between B_1 and the several criteria are positive. In three of the seven scales, the differentiation between high and low groups is statistically significant. B_2, B_4, C_1, and C_2 show essentially this same pattern — zero or positive relationships with the criterion. B_3 tends to be positively correlated with performance criteria and is so to a marked extent in Sample C, the group of women bank tellers. The four B scales and the two C scales appear to describe adaptive characteristics as far as success on the job is concerned.

Characteristically, N_1, N_2, and N_3 are negatively correlated with work performance. N_1 is negatively correlated with performance in six of the seven samples, and significantly so in two. N_2 is negatively correlated with performance in all seven samples, and significantly so in four. N_3 is negatively correlated with performance in all seven samples, and significantly so in two. These correlations suggest that spiritlessness, apprehensiveness, and aggression are nonadaptive characteristics as far as success on the job is concerned.

A_1, the measure of hyperactivity, shows little predictive validity and, in addition, does not exhibit the kind of consistency across samples noted in the B, C, and N scales. A_2, the measure of egocentricity, exhibits essentially the same pattern. A_1 and A_2 may well exemplify characteristics that are differentially adaptive or nonadaptive, depending on what other traits occur with them and on the kind of job a person holds.

PREDICTIVE VALIDITIES OF THE
FIVE MOTIVATION FACTORS

Before describing the predictive validities of the motivation factors, let us consider the manner in which the scales defining the factors were combined to produce quantitative factor scores. For the purpose of examining the factor validities, it was decided to work with the factors as defined subsequent to the set of oblique rotations described in the preceding chapter.

The drive factor (D) is loaded positively on B_1 and B_4 and negatively on N_3. A simple weighting system was devised, based on the ratios of the squares of the factor loadings before the oblique rotations to the standard deviations of the scales. In some cases a constant was added to place the lower limit of the factor score at zero. The drive factor, then, is defined as follows:

$$\text{Drive} = 2B_1 + B_4 - 3N_1 + 45.$$

The score range on this factor is from 0 to 116.

The achievement factor subsequent to the oblique rotations had positive loadings on B_2, B_4, and A_2. Deriving a set of weights by the procedure just described defines this factor as follows:

$$\text{Achievement} = \frac{(2B_2 + 2B_4 + 3A_2)}{2}$$

The division by two simply reduces the range and makes the factor scores easier to work with. The range on the achievement factor is from 0 to 83.

The status factor subsequent to oblique rotations is loaded positively on B_2, C_1, C_2, and A_1. Deriving a set of weights by the procedure described earlier defines this factor as follows:

$$\text{Status} = \frac{(B_2 + C_1 + 2C_2 + 2A_1)}{2}$$

Again, the division by two was made to make the scores easier to manipulate. The obtainable factor score range on the status factor is 0 to 53.

The anxiety factor subsequent to the oblique rotations is loaded positively on A_1, A_2, N_1, and N_2 and negatively on B_4. Deriving a set of weights by the procedure described earlier defines this factor as follows:

$$\text{Anxiety} = \frac{(2A_1 + 3A_2 + 3N_1 + 2N_2 - 2B_4 + 54)}{2}$$

The obtainable factor score range on the anxiety factor is from 0 to 149.

The aggression factor subsequent to the oblique rotations is loaded positively on N_3 and negatively on B_3. A set of weights, obtainable as described earlier, defines this factor as follows:

$$\text{Aggression} = N_3 - 2B_3 + 46.$$

The obtainable factor score range on the aggression factor is 0 to 84.

The validities of these five factors were obtained by means of the same statistical operations used with the motivation scales. However, rather than present this information in the form of tables as was done earlier, essentially the same information is shown by means of a set of five figures (Exhibits 40 through 44). These figures show, for each of the job groups, the arithmetic mean of the "high" criterion group; the mean of the "low" criterion group; the serial correlation describing the strength of the relationship between the factor and the criterion, where appropriate; and an indication of whether the high and low groups can be differentiated significantly by the factor score at least at the .05 level of significance. This form of presentation has the advantage of locating both criterion groups on the factor scale and permitting comparisons among the several job groups.

The Drive Factor

Exhibit 40 shows this information relative to the drive factor. It is immediately apparent from this figure that there are sizable differences among the job groups in the way men and women describe themselves. The technical managers, the securities salesmen, and the group of technical salesmen see themselves as having a sizable amount of directed energy or channeled drive. The hourly production and maintenance workers, by contrast, occupy a much lower position on the scale; the average of the high hourly workers does not approach the average of the low criterion groups of the three other job groups just mentioned. The high and low women bank tellers show some overlap with these hourly production and maintenance workers. Public utility operators occupy an intermediate position on the drive factor scale.

All the serial correlation coefficients shown are positive, the largest being +.60. In the case of three of these groups — the technical managers, the securities salesmen, and the industrial sales group — the differentiation between high and low groups is significant at least at the .05 level. The marked discrepancy between the men in the top job groups and those in the bottom groups on this characteristic suggests that they are quite

EXHIBIT 40

Means of High and Low Criterion Groups in a Variety
of Jobs — Biserial or Point Biserial Coefficients Showing
Strength of the Correlation with the Criterion — Drive Factor

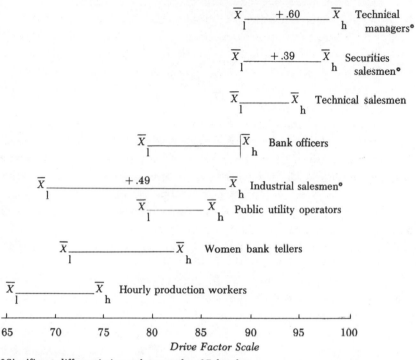

Drive Factor Scale

*Significant differentiation at least at the .05 level.

different, motivationally speaking, and may explain in part why they have difficulty communicating or being tolerant of one another.

It was suggested earlier that a motivational characteristic like the one defined here should have predictive validity across all job groups in industry, since it is a generally adaptive human characteristic. The data shown in Exhibit 40 suggest that this may be true, but a rigorous test of the significance of this hypothesis is needed to be certain.

A statistical technique, the "analysis of variance," permits the performance of three kinds of statistical tests concurrently; one kind tests the hypothesis just stated. A second hypothesis — that the job groups differ significantly from one another — can also be tested. Finally, we can test the hypothesis that the factor has differential predictive validity for the several job groups. This hypothesis tests for what is technically called an interaction effect.

Exhibit E-1 in Appendix E shows the results of an analysis of variance done on the data shown graphically in Exhibit 40. In the exhibits in Appendix E, the first column specifies the *source* of the variability or kind of difference. There are four of these: The first is associated with differences between the two criterion groups; the second is associated with variation among the eight job groups; the third is associated with the criterion group/job group interaction; and the fourth gives individual differences within each of the 16 criterion group/job group combinations. This fourth source is assumed to be random variation and is used to evaluate the significance of the other three. The other three columns are labeled *MS*, *F*, and *p*, respectively.

The estimates of the total variance coming from the several sources are obtained by dividing the sum of the squared deviations from the mean (*SS*) by the indicated number of degrees of freedom (*df*). These are given in the *MS* column. If all four of these are approximately the same size, none of the sources is producing nonrandom variability; that is, there are no significant differences between criterion groups, job groups, or interaction combinations. Notice that in Exhibit E-1 the *MS*'s associated with the criterion groups and the job groups are sizably larger than the other two.

The *F* values are obtained by dividing the *MS* of one of the sources (for example, job groups) by the estimate of random variability — the within-groups source.

The probability of getting an *F* value as large as or larger than the one observed by chance or as a result of random errors of sampling is indicated by the *p* column. The *p* value of $<.01$ in the row labeled "criterion groups" simply means that the probability of getting an *F* value of 7.63 or larger under these conditions is less than 1 in 100. The *F* value, then, is significant at the .01 level.

Three conclusions may be drawn from Exhibit E-1. First, there are significant differences between high and low criterion groups across the collection of job groups. The drive factor, in general, has predictive validity. Second, there are highly significant differences among the eight job groups. The drive factor is differentially represented in groups of employed men and women in different kinds of jobs in different companies. Different jobs have different drive requirements. Third, when the effects of the first two sources are removed, there are insignificant differences among the 16 company/criterion group combinations. This last finding, of course, strengthens the first two conclusions.

The Achievement Factor

Exhibit 41 presents information on the validity of the achievement factor. Here again, the means of the high and low criterion groups are shown for each of eight job groups. This figure differs somewhat from the preceding one, particularly with regard to the arrangement of job groups on the achievement scale. All three groups of salesmen, the technical managers, and the bank officers describe themselves as having a fair amount of this characteristic. The means of the low criterion groups in each of these five job groups are higher than the means of the high criterion groups in the other three job groups. The two job groups of hourly paid men and the group of women not only run low on this scale but show little differentiation between high and low criterion groups. A reversal in direction may be noted in the cases of the securities salesmen and the public utility employees. The technical managers and the industrial salesmen show evidence of significant predictive validity on this scale. How-

EXHIBIT 41

Means of High and Low Criterion Groups in a Variety of Jobs — Biserial or Point Biserial Coefficients Showing Strength of the Correlation with the Criterion — Achievement Factor

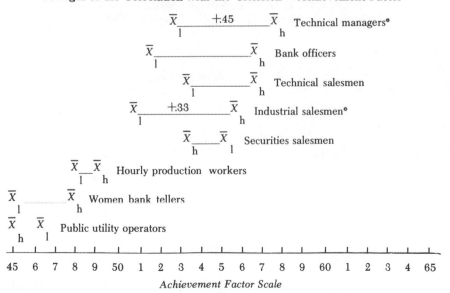

Achievement Factor Scale

*Significant differentiation at least at the .05 level.

ever, differences among job groups appear to be more marked than differences between criterion groups.

Exhibit E-2 presents the analysis of variance on the data shown in Exhibit 41. Here differences between criterion groups are significant at the .05 level and variation among job groups is significant at the .001 level. Again, as in Exhibit E-1, the interaction effect is not a significant source of variation. The conclusion can be drawn from this that the achievement factor significantly differentiates between people judged high or low on work performance across the samples used here. Similarly, it may be concluded that different jobs in different companies have different "achievement" requirements or attract men and women with different strengths of the achievement need.

The Status Factor

Exhibit 42 shows the validity data for the status factor. This motivational characteristic, as one might expect, is descriptive of the three groups

EXHIBIT 42

**Means of High and Low Criterion Groups in a Variety.
of Jobs — Biserial or Point Biserial Coefficients Showing
Strength of the Correlation with the Criterion — Status Factor**

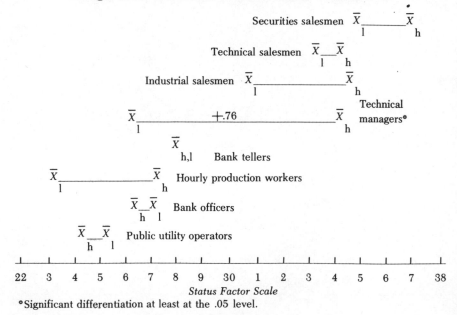

*Significant differentiation at least at the .05 level.

of salesmen and the successful technical managers. The group of technical managers is an interesting one; the high criterion group is comparable to the technical and industrial salesmen and the low criterion group is comparable to the bank tellers, bank officers, hourly production workers, and hourly public utility operators. Neither the hourly paid men nor the two groups of bank employees appear to have this characteristic at all well developed. Only the group of technical managers shows statistically significant differentiation between men judged to be "high" and those judged to be "low" in work performance and managerial potential.

The analysis of variance done on the data shown in Exhibit 42 is presented in Exhibit E-3. It is again apparent in Exhibit E-3 that highly significant differences among job groups exist and, somewhat surprisingly, differences between high and low criterion groups are significant at the .05 level. That this is probably a function of two or three of the job groups is suggested by the fact that the interaction effects are sizable even though not statistically significant. The conclusion to be drawn here is that different jobs place differential demands on people relative to this type of motivation, and this type of motivation is positively correlated with job performance — for at least certain types of jobs.

The Anxiety Factor

Exhibit 43 shows the validity data for the anxiety factor. Several things are immediately apparent here. First, the correlation between scores on this factor and job performance is negative rather than positive. In the case of two of these job groups, women bank tellers and technical managers, the differentiation between high and low criterion groups is statistically significant. Note that the successful technical managers, public utility operators, securities salesmen, and the group of technical salesmen are nonreactors in the anxiety dimension. They take the minor pressures and stresses of work in stride.

One of the more interesting job groups shown here is that of bank officers. This group consists of 30 men seen by PSP for general evaluation. From performance ratings made by their superiors, 10 could be assigned to an outstanding group, 20 to a satisfactory group. Although not immediately apparent from this exhibit, these men show anxiety scores that are neither very high nor very low, and, as can be seen, this is the only group in which the high group has a higher factor score than does the low group.

EXHIBIT 43

Means of High and Low Criterion Groups in a Variety of Jobs — Biserial or Point Biserial Coefficients Showing Strength of the Correlation with the Criterion — Anxiety Factor

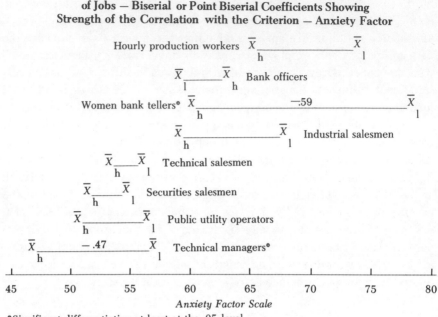

Anxiety Factor Scale

°Significant differentiation at least at the .05 level.

There is a suggestion here that hourly paid workers in industry are higher on this scale than are salaried people. This is another motivation differential that may make it difficult for management and labor to understand each other.

The analysis of variance performed on the data in Exhibit 43 is shown as Exhibit E-4. Differences between criterion groups across all samples are significant at the .05 level; and job group differences are significant at the .001 level. The anxiety factor, then, differentially characterizes high and low performers on the job, and sizable differences exist among job groups on this factor.

The Aggression Factor

Exhibit 44 shows the validity data for the aggression factor. Two of the job groups contain high and low performers significantly differentiated from one another on this factor. Not only do the hourly production workers run higher on this factor as a group, but the men in the low

EXHIBIT 44

**Means of High and Low Criterion Groups in a Variety
of Jobs — Biserial or Point Biserial Coefficients Showing
Strength of the Correlation with the Criterion — Aggression Factor**

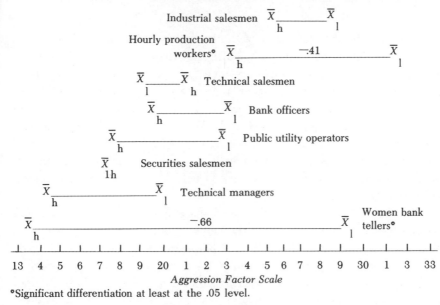

Aggression Factor Scale

°Significant differentiation at least at the .05 level.

criterion group have the highest average aggression score in the entire collection of job groups. The significant difference between the high and low performers among the women bank tellers is also quite dramatic. The high group shows the least amount of this characteristic of any job group, but the low-rated bank tellers are the second highest. This, then, is a highly nonadaptive characteristic in women on this job.

The three groups of salesmen are quite divergent on this characteristic. The securities salesmen show little of it; the industrial sales group shows quite a bit. Notice that the public utility operators appear to run somewhat higher on this factor than they do on the anxiety factor. Reacting with anxiety is quite nonadaptive, but a certain amount of aggression may be tolerated in this kind of work. The securities salesmen and the technical managers responded infrequently either with anxiety or with aggression to minor irritations on the job.

Exhibit E-5 shows the analysis of variance done on the data in Exhibit 44. Differences between high and low criterion groups across the board are significant at the .01 level, and differences between job groups are again significant at the .001 level. For the first time a significant interaction effect may be noted. Aggression appears to be differentially related to job performance in the several job groups being looked at here.

Summary of the Validity Data for the Factor Scales

A somewhat different view of the predictive validities of these scales is shown in Exhibits 45 and 46. The first of these shows the high group averages for each of the samples of men and women for whom we have performance criteria. The group averages have been converted into their percentile rank equivalents, the norm group being a 25 percent random sample of the men originally used in the Hackman Job Satisfaction Schedule item analysis. These groups, then, are being compared to salaried men in industry. Since the averages are based on successful groups of men and women, it is of some interest to note where they fall in comparison to salaried men in general.

On the drive factor all groups, with the exception of the hourly laborers (A), are near the median of the norm group or markedly above it. Three of the samples — the technical managers (D), the technical salesmen (E), and the securities salesmen (G) — average well above the median of the norm group. Either men with this kind of drive are the only ones who seek out jobs of this type or men who have this kind of drive are the only ones successful at this kind of work. That the first explanation is probably true is attested by the information in Exhibit 46, which shows a similar presentation of averages for the low criterion groups. Note that the groups coming from samples G, D, and E also have averages above the norm group median. The low groups in samples B, F, and H average out at or below the median, which supports the second explanation.

It may be noted that on the achievement factor the high criterion groups in five of the job samples average above the median of the norm group, while the high criterion groups in three of the samples average well below the median of the norm group. This suggests that achievement motivation is either quite characteristic or quite uncharacteristic of people seeking out certain types of jobs. The technical managers (D), the bank officers (H), the technical salesmen (E), the industrial salesmen (F), and the securities salesmen (G) show this trait; the industrial laborers (A), the women bank tellers (C), and the public utility operators (B) do not.

If Exhibit 45 is contrasted with Exhibit 46 it may be seen that the separation observed in the high groups is not as marked as it is in the

EXHIBIT 45

Position of High Criterion Groups
on Standard Norms — Motivation Factors

Job Groups

A — Industrial laborers
B — Public utility operators
C — Women bank tellers
D — Technical managers
E — Technical salesmen
F — Industrial salesmen
G — Securities salesmen
H — Bank officers

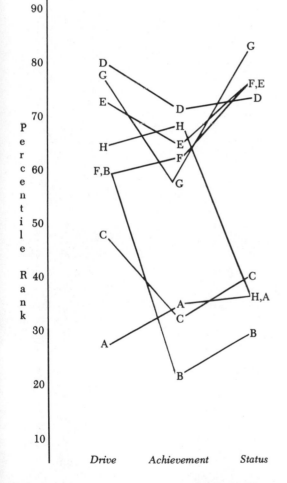

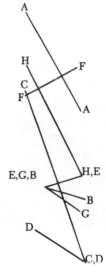

Drive   Achievement   Status   Anxiety   Aggression

Motivation Factors

EXHIBIT 46

Position of Low Criterion Groups
on Standard Norms — Motivation Factors

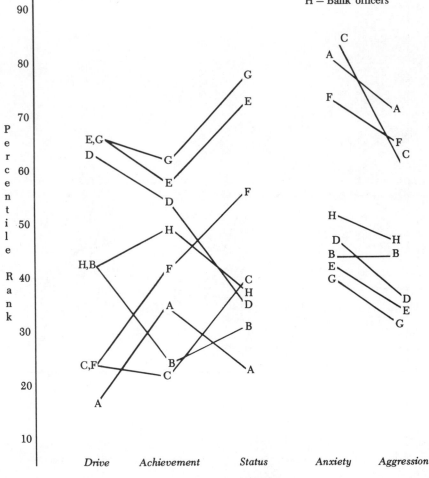

Job Groups

A — Industrial laborers
B — Public utility operators
C — Women bank tellers
D — Technical managers
E — Technical salesmen
F — Industrial salesmen
G — Securities salesmen
H — Bank officers

low criterion groups. The low groups in samples H, D, E, and G still average at or above the median of the norm group; the low group in sample F (industrial salesmen) is below the median, and A, B, and C low groups occupy approximately the same low positions on the norm scale. The motivational characteristic measured by the achievement factor may be more typical of people seeking out certain kinds of jobs than of people differentially successful on them.

A somewhat similar state of affairs exists in connection with the status factor. This type of motivation characterizes both high and low criterion groups in the sample of securities salesmen (G) and in the sample of technical salesmen (E). However, in the case of Samples F and D the high groups show this characteristic to a marked degree and the low groups show it to a lesser degree. The women bank tellers (C), the bank officers (H), the industrial laborers (A), and the public utility operators (B) do not have a great deal of this type of motivation in their make-ups.

Four of the high job groups — E, G, B, and D — average out low on the anxiety factor. Another four high criterion groups — A, H, C, and F — average out at the median or somewhat above. Both high and low groups from Samples C, A, and F tend to run high anxiety factor scores. Apparently a fair amount of this trait can be tolerated in these jobs. All low criterion groups, irrespective of job sample, run somewhat higher anxiety scores.

A similar picture characterizes the averages of these high and low criterion groups on the aggression factor. The hourly paid industrial workers (A) and the group of industrial salesmen (F) show elevated aggression scores. The securities salesmen (G), the technical managers (D), the bank officers (H), the public utility operators (B), and the technical salesmen (E) show relatively low average aggression scores.

To summarize the significance of these data on the predictive validities of the motivation factors, it appears that the drive factor is generally adaptive as far as work is concerned. As a motivational trait, it may be more characteristic of men and women at the upper end of the occupational hierarchy than at the lower end. The anxiety factor is generally nonadaptive as far as work is concerned, and it appears to be more typical of people at the lower end of the occupational hierarchy than the upper end. The tendency to respond aggressively to minor irritants would seem to be generally nonadaptive and apparently quite nonadaptive in some kinds of jobs.

The two motivation factors that specify the direction in which motivation is channeled — achievement and status — do not appear to have the same kind of general significance. Both are characteristic of successful men and women in some jobs, but they are not at all characteristic of men and women in other jobs. In fact, they may be nonadaptive characteristics for continuing success and satisfaction in some kinds of work.

Of course, it comes as no surprise to rediscover that a *pattern* of motivational characteristics differentiates successful and satisfied men and women in industry from those not quite so fortunate.

8

Theoretical Implications
for Work Motivation

CHAPTER 7 COMPLETED THE DESCRIPTION of the research on work motivation in which Psychological Service of Pittsburgh has been engaged since 1958. One of its missions was accomplished: the development of a system for describing and measuring the work motivation of individuals. However, the research has implications beyond this practical end product, and this chapter considers the contributions to work motivation theory generated by the study.

It should be remembered that what has been described is motivation for work and that there has been no presumption to describe all forms of motivation characteristic of adult men and women. In addition, the concept of motivation presented here attempts to explain why men and women work at their jobs and is not directly concerned with the way they learn their jobs.

There are two levels at which the problem of developing a theory of work motivation can be attacked. The first level is essentially psychological in that it purports to describe the functioning of an adult in a complicated social milieu, and the description is essentially on a behavioral level. The second level is broadly biological in that it purports to make the behavioral hypotheses consistent with facts or conjectures about the function of the human nervous system and the body that houses it.

Many psychologists and informed laymen are satisfied with the psychological explanations; others prefer extensions into the biological realm.

PSYCHOLOGICAL HYPOTHESES

At the behavioral level there are five kinds of information to work with: (1) the interrelations among feelings and job conditions found in the reanalysis of Herzberg's interview data; (2) the interrelations among feelings and job conditions specified by the factor analyses done on data collected in an attitude survey; (3) the relationships between the motivation factors derived from the Hackman Job Satisfaction Schedule and the responses of men and women to individual items in the Guilford-Zimmerman Temperament Survey; (4) the interrelations among the 11 motivation scales developed from the G-ZTS; (5) the relationships between these same motivation scales and measures of success at work. Each kind of information generates hypotheses about work motivation.

The Herzberg Data

As described earlier, the interview method used by Herzberg produced two basic types of data. The men interviewed reported job conditions that resulted in general satisfaction or dissatisfaction with work. They also reported specific kinds of feeling experiences that accompanied these job conditions.

Relatively few satisfaction-producing job conditions were reported with any frequency, suggesting that there really are not many kinds of things at work that can generate satisfaction. More dissatisfaction-producing job conditions were reported, and, with few exceptions, these were qualitatively different from those reported as producing satisfaction.

The feelings reported by these men were particularly significant.

When talking about happy episodes they not only reported general satisfaction but also used such words as accomplishment, responsibility, recognition, and growth to describe how they felt. When talking about unhappy episodes, they not only reported dissatisfaction but also used words such as anger, disgust, anxiety, frustration, and insecurity to describe how they felt.

The data strongly suggest that the positive feelings have motivational significance, and the kind of motivation characterizing a man can be inferred from the feeling words he uses in describing such an experience. A man who does not report his feeling in such words either is not motivated or is not having his motivation reinforced by conditions on the job.

Words about unhappy episodes — for example, anger and anxiety — describe states of emotional tension, and the kind of tension can be inferred from the choice of words. A man reporting many of these words is interpreting conditions and events on his job as generally threatening or irritating. A man reporting few of them is a nonreactor in an emotional sense, at least as far as his job is concerned.

The fact that qualitatively different kinds of feeling words accompany happy and unhappy episodes supports this two-factor hypothesis. The additional fact that the collection of job conditions that produces happy states is different from the collection that produces unhappy states furnishes added support. *Good organization of work* is not reported as producing motivationally significant feelings accompanying satisfaction, but *poor organization of work* is frequently reported as producing emotional tension accompanying dissatisfaction. The only kind of supervision that produces motivationally significant feelings is *permissive supervision*. Any other form — critical, unfriendly, incompetent — produces negative emotional reactions in these men.

A second hypothesis can be generated from these data: Job conditions producing motivationally significant feelings reinforce adaptive work behavior and attitudes and serve the useful function of maintaining or augmenting work effectiveness. Job conditions generating emotional tension produce nonadaptive work behavior and attitudes and serve to reduce work effectiveness.

A third hypothesis follows from these two: Eliminating the job conditions that produce dissatisfaction will end the dissatisfaction but will have little or no motivational significance for the man involved. This is like saying that if a man normally works at 40 percent efficiency, but for a time is working at 30 percent because of job irritants, eliminating the irritants may return him to 40 percent efficiency, but will not move him beyond that point. For some men dissatisfaction is a way of life. These men will find something to be irritated by, no matter what the situation.

Attempts to relate the feelings associated with pleasant episodes to the job conditions producing them revealed some rather startling relationships. Two clusters of feelings and events appeared. The first consisted of feelings of recognition, confidence, and accomplishment produced by interesting work, permissive supervision, successful completion of a task, and praise. The second consisted of feelings of status, responsibility, and growth produced by interesting work, supervisory responsibility, and a promotion. Two other feelings, financial progress and security, were produced by different patterns of job conditions with partially overlapping elements.

These relationships suggest that motivation for work is channeled into two kinds of work activity. The first activity is tied to the specific skills developed and used by a man in doing his job, and his primary satisfaction comes from closure experiences; that is, successfully completing a task. The feeling word *accomplishment* describes this type of motivation. The second is tied to the activities involved in interacting with other people on the job. Men having the first type are *task*-oriented; men having the second type are *situation*-oriented; both are *work-activity-oriented*. Work is interesting and challenging to them.

Feelings of security and financial progress do not fit either of these two clusters and are produced by job conditions that are not tied to work. Hence it follows that some men view work as a necessary evil; for example, as a means to some other end. Money will buy a lot of experiences that are outside work. Men who report these feelings and reinforcing conditions, rather than those in the two clusters, deny the stimulation value of work itself.

The Attitude Survey Data

Chapter 3 reported a series of factor analyses performed on the intercorrelations among the several positive feeling words and reinforcing job conditions. These feelings and conditions were presented in a structured questionnaire as an integral part of an attitude survey and were responded to in the same way as were the other questions in the survey. Intercorrelation matrices were constructed from the responses given by four groups of employees. Each of the four matrices was then factor analyzed.

Three clusters of feelings and job conditions occurred in all four solutions. A fourth cluster occurred in three of them. In each solution each variable exhibited sizable loadings on or correlated with the first factor, with a few feelings and job conditions very highly loaded on or correlated with this general factor. The significant feelings and job conditions in this first factor were the same as those in the task-oriented or accomplishment cluster found in the Herzberg data.

The second factor consisted of a cluster of feelings and job conditions that duplicated the social or situation-oriented cluster found in the Herzberg data, but with some variation from it. The third factor consisted of the cluster of extrinsic reinforcing events and conditions showing up in the Herzberg data, together with a set of feeling words that partially overlapped the two clusters appearing in the Herzberg data. The fourth factor was a variant of the accomplishment or task-oriented cluster.

Attempts to factor matrices of intercorrelations among the feeling words accompanying unhappy episodes and the job conditions producing them met with little success. Meaningful clusters of feelings and job conditions did not emerge from these analyses. This result, then, in a sense supports the hypothesis that here is a kind of experience quite different from the one represented by a happy episode.

Additional insight into the significance of the four factors or clusters of feelings and job conditions can be obtained by going to a slightly different kind of interpretive analysis. The basis for the analysis is illustrated in Exhibit A-3 in Appendix A. From this exhibit were identified the feelings or job conditions that have the same factor structure. For example, a promotion loads on Factors T_2 and T_3, and no other variable shows this pattern. It therefore has a unique factor structure. However, permissive supervision, interesting work, successful completion of a task, and a feeling of confidence all load on factors T_1 and T_4. Supervision of others, work of subordinates, and a feeling of responsibility all load on factor T_2 alone. This method of identifying combinations of variables was followed throughout the set of four factor patterns.

The variables with consistent factor structures in all four patterns distribute themselves into three informative clusters of feelings and job conditions. The first cluster consists of the following:

Feelings: Accomplishment
     Confidence
     Pride
     Recognition

Job Conditions: Interesting and challenging work
      Permissive supervision
      Successful completion of a task
      Praise.

Herzberg's data suggested that three of these feelings could be arranged in a hierarchy: recognition, confidence, and accomplishment. In these factor patterns praise went most frequently with recognition; successful completion of a task and permissive supervision, with confidence; and interesting and challenging work, with accomplishment. This again suggests that the words an individual uses to express his feelings when his motivation is reinforced on the job reflect not only the type of motivation characterizing him but also the level of motivational maturity he has reached. A man at the lowest level needs praise as a reinforcing agent. A man reporting confidence is reinforced by being allowed to do a job in his own way and by closure experiences. A man at the highest level of motivational maturity has his skills so well developed that all he needs is a situation in which to exercise them: that is, interesting and challenging work.

The second cluster coming out of this analysis is as follows:

Feelings: Responsibility
              Personal growth

Job Conditions: Supervision of others
                  Good work by subordinates.

In these factor patterns a feeling of responsibility always accompanied supervision of others. However, a feeling of personal growth was produced by other agents, too — for example, a raise or a promotion. In some of the factor patterns, supervision of others and good work by subordinates are accompanied by feelings of accomplishment and status.

The invariant nature of the one source of a feeling of responsibility — being given supervision over others — suggests that men exhibiting this pattern are active *responsibility seekers* and, at one level of motivational development, get their job satisfaction from assuming responsibility for more and more people and activities. At a higher level of sophistication or maturity, these same men require for their reinforcement not only responsibility for people per se but good performance from them. This is tantamount to saying that a supervisor of the first level likes his job and his subordinates no matter what they do or how they perform. A man on the second level enjoys his subordinates if they produce for him, and he actively seeks ways to develop them so that they will produce. The developmental progression hypothesized here may account for a well-known phenomenon — the inability of many good first-line supervisors to delegate responsibility or to handle and derive satisfaction from movement up the managerial ladder. Such a person would appear to be fixated on the lower level.

The third cluster is as follows:

    Feelings: Security
                   Financial progress
                   Importance
                   Acceptance

    Job Conditions: A promotion
                      A raise
                      Increased status.

Two things characterize this pattern. First, the job conditions are extrinsic to the work activity itself. Second, the feelings reflect three of the four meanings ordinarily attached to the word "security." These data, then, support the hypothesis previously defined, that man works not because he enjoys it but for rewards extrinsic to the work activity itself.

There is no one word to describe this kind of motivation. In a sense these people are *security seekers*, since for them security is vested in money, social acceptance, or social status. It may be hypothesized that they represent levels in a security hierarchy with the feeling words acceptance, financial progress, and importance defining the progression from the lowest to the highest level.

The factor analyses reported in Chapter 3 showed that a feeling of security accompanied the accomplishment cluster in several of the factor patterns. Security, then, is also vested in the specific skills a man has, and these feelings are reinforced by praise and successful completion of a task. Security is also a function of what a man can *do* as well as what he has.

Many of these positive feeling words do not have an opposite. What is the opposite of accomplishment, responsibility, or growth? On the other hand, security has an opposite: insecurity. The opposite of acceptance is rejection, and the opposite of importance is unimportance. This suggests again that the kind of motivation represented by the first two clusters is quite different from the kind represented by the third. A man can identify with and enjoy work activity for its own sake or he can view work as a means to an end.

These clusters differ in another sense. Feelings of insecurity, rejection, and unimportance reflect emotional tension and are variants of anxiety reactions on the part of these men. Security seekers may respond apprehensively to their environments and may work to remove, or at least reduce, the effectiveness of the environmental agents that generate this kind of tension.

The Motivation Scales

Item analyses of the G-ZTS for groups of men checking many or a few of the elements of the HJSS accomplishment, social, and money-status patterns yielded three sets of items that could be further differentiated into more homogeneous subsets. Two such subsets of items occurred in the accomplishment analysis, four in the social analysis, and two in the money-status analysis. Since the G-ZTS asks a person to describe himself by reacting to these questions, a man answering these items in the keyed direction is describing himself in terms of personality or temperament traits that go along with, or are characteristic of, men with a great deal of the type of motivation under scrutiny.

Men exhibiting the accomplishment pattern describe themselves as hyperactive and egocentric. Men exhibiting the social pattern describe themselves as industrious, socially aggressive, tolerant, and serious minded Men exhibiting the money-status pattern describe themselves as both deferent and authoritative.

Two things that were not anticipated stand out strikingly in this set of relationships. The first is the appearance of two sets of items that reflect a man's level of activation; these differ in a significant fashion. One scale describes a person who is energetic, vigorous, and industrious, who not only has a great deal of energy but has that energy harnessed and directed toward useful activity. A person with this kind of energy does not waste it in idle activity; his energy is directed. The other scale describes a person who is hyperactive and whose energy is not harnessed or directed but appears to be of the free-floating variety.

This suggests that the intrinsically motivated man has a great deal of physical energy that he can and does mobilize to aid and abet his stimulation seeking. This energy appears to be of two types. We can hypothesize that directed energy is a generally adaptive characteristic of men with strong responsibility drives, while the free-floating type of energy is characteristic of men with strong accomplishment drives that may or may not be adaptive in specific types of work.

The second thing that is peculiarly striking in these data is this: The adaptive characteristics that industry looks for in an employee describe the situation-oriented, responsibility-seeking man. It seems reasonable to assume, then, that responsibility-seeking motivation is generally adaptive in the work situation and that men with this type of motivation are likely to be successful at any kind of industrial work.

The two C scales, C_1 and C_2, emerged from the contrasting of high money-status and low money-status men. They describe men who are sociable, deferent, and admiring on the one hand and assertive, authoritative, and domineering on the other. These scales describe men who are adept at playing two kinds of social roles, the deferent and the dominant. Men with these traits, then, are in a sense manipulators of people and of social situations. They appear to be means-ends people in that work to them is a means to some extrinsic end, be it money, social acceptance, or status. A person with this kind of motivation might be described as an *instrumentalist*.

It should be remembered that these scales describe people with just one particular kind of motivation. The sizable correlation among the three HJSS factors and the difficulties in getting matched high A/low A, high B/low B, and high C/low C factor samples suggest that motivations of these types occur in patterns in men; and rarely in industry would we find a man who is only a closure seeker, a responsibility seeker, or an instrumentalist.

When G-ZTS item responses of men with high and low negative factor scores were contrasted, a set of three scales emerged. On the first of these a man describes himself as spiritless and lacking in energy. On the second he sees himself as anxiety ridden and apprehensive. On the third he describes himself as aggressive, pugnacious, and resentful. The second and third describe characteristic ways of responding to everyday irritations and pressures on the job. Their appearance in this context strongly supports a previously stated hypothesis that men reporting extensive dissatisfaction with work are people who respond emotionally, rather than intellectually, to their jobs. The fact that these men are also spiritless and lethargic strongly supports the hypothesis that responding in any of these three ways is nonadaptive as far as work is concerned. These ways of responding interfere with effective work, and men with these characteristics tend to perform below standard on their jobs.

Interrelationships Among the Motivation Scales

The interrelationships among the 11 scales can be looked at in any of three ways. First, there is some built-in correlation among them because a few items contribute to more than one scale; that is, they occur in more than one subset. They may be keyed the same or opposite, thus producing positive or negative correlations. Second, some of the scales consistently correlate positively or negatively with one another for the groups of people on whom we have motivation-scale data. Third, intercorrelation matrices constructed from motivation scale data on a variety of work groups have been factor analyzed, and the resulting factor patterns can be examined for similarities or differences.

If we consider the first way of looking at these interrelationships, we note that three of the four B scales correlate negatively with the three N scales in a fixed pattern. B_1 correlates negatively with N_1; men who describe themselves as energetic and industrious deny that they are spiritless and lacking in energy. B_3 correlates negatively with N_3; men who see themselves as friendly and tolerant deny that they are pugnacious and resentful. B_4 correlates negatively with N_2; men who conceive of themselves as serious minded, organized, and confident do not think that they are anxiety ridden and apprehensive. The negative correlations between B_3 and N_3 and between B_4 and N_2 suggest that the pressures and irritations of a job are primarily people-tied. Not only are people a major source of reinforcement (stimulation) for responsibility seekers, but they are a major source of emotional tension.

The pattern of intercorrelations among the 11 motivation scales can be seen in the results of factor analyses to be discussed presently. However, one set of intercorrelations among these scales is of interest here. N_2, the measure of anxiety, and N_3, the measure of aggression, are positively correlated, suggesting that the tendency to respond emotionally is a general trait. However, the pattern of correlations between each of these two and the remaining nine scales is different. Of peculiar significance is the fact that N_3 does not correlate negatively with B_1 and B_2, suggesting that a tendency to respond aggressively and pugnaciously may be characteristic of some men who have high directed energy levels and a great deal of social aggressiveness in their make-up and, hence, may be adaptive in some kinds of jobs. Anxiety and apprehensiveness appear to be generally nonadaptive in any work setting.

As was pointed out earlier, the intercorrelations among the 11 motivation scales were calculated on data drawn from 12 quite different groups of men and women. Each of the 12 matrices was factor analyzed, and the resulting factor patterns were transformed to other patterns satisfying the criteria of simple structure. Each of the intercorrelation matrices could be accounted for or described by four factors. Two of the factors occurred in all 12 samples, one occurred in 11 of the 12, one occurred in 6 samples, and one occurred in 7 samples. Five separate and statistically independent clusters of scales then came out of the analysis.

These *identical clusters* came out of a factor analysis of the correlation matrix containing the average correlations across 11 of the 12 samples. In view of this, it can be said that work motivation is describable by one simple system, irrespective of whether the people being described are men or women, salaried or hourly paid, about to enter the job market or well established in a career.

Motivated people at work can be described in terms of these five dimensions:

1. The amount of directed energy or sheer drive they have.
2. The extent to which they are identified with work in a social context that yields closure experiences.
3. The extent to which they view work solely as a means to some end or goal extrinsic to the work itself.
4. The extent to which ordinary pressures of work are threatening and generate anxiety reactions.
5. The extent to which the ordinary pressures of work generate aggressive and pugnacious reactions.

It seems to follow that highly motivated men and women characteristically maintain a high level of directed energy at work. These people work for the satisfaction inherent in the work activity itself or, alternatively, work to achieve ends or goals extrinsic to the work. Typically, they are not threatened or irritated by the routine pressures of a job.

It is easy to slip into the habit of thinking about people as though they fit just one of the dimensions described above. To repeat, such pure types probably do not exist. People have combinations of these traits, and describing a man or woman with this system should be done in terms of a pattern or profile rather than a single-dimension typing. These five factors are correlated: the first three positively with each other, the last two positively with each other, and the first three negatively with the last two.

Relationships Between the Motivation Scales and Criteria of Success on the Job

The data presented in Chapter 7 show the relationships between the several motivation scales, the factors derived from them, and criteria of success on some jobs. The four B scales are positively related to success at work, at least in these job settings. Hyperactivity and egocentricity are differentially correlated with success, depending upon the type of job a man has. The three N scales, measuring spiritlessness, anxiety, and aggression, are as a rule negatively correlated with success on the job. These results, then, support several of the hypotheses derived from other analyses.

The motivation scales, when they do differentiate among criterion groups, sort out the outstanding performers. This suggests that these measures of motivation are more useful in identifying high-level performers than in identifying poor or inadequate performers, but this does not exclude the possibility of using them in an elimination system.

The predictive validities associated with the five motivation factors permit additional hypotheses about motivation for work. Since the *drive* factor is generally valid in predicting success on the job, it must be assumed that a certain amount of directed or harnessed energy is required for success on any job, even though its absolute requirement may vary from job to job. This hypothesis does not hold for the *achievement* and *status* factors. The data suggest that specific jobs have quite different requirements as to status and achievement motivation. People whose status and achievement motivation is high may find some kinds of work distasteful and, basically, nonreinforcing. By the same token, some jobs require men with these kinds of motivation, and the lack of either may preclude success on them.

Finally, the characteristics measured by the anxiety and aggression factors are nonadaptive in most jobs but can be tolerated in some to a greater extent than in others. Such reactions are tolerated to a greater extent in women than in men and to a greater extent in hourly workers than in salaried personnel.

SUMMARY

The preceding discussion has summarized many of the hypotheses that can be generated about motivation for work. The theory emerging from the data suggests that motivation for work involves two quite different kinds of mediating systems. One of these systems is descriptive of the way in which work itself generates satisfaction and reinforces a person's basic stimulation needs. The other system describes the way in which work is used as an instrumentality for achieving rewards unrelated to work itself. Both types of motivation are adaptive, but differentially so, depending on the type of job an individual has or is seeking.

One of the reasons for collecting these data and analyzing them was to develop a method of measuring work motivation in individuals. Even though the scales developed in conjunction with the item analyses leave something to be desired as far as reliability is concerned, one now knows how to develop other items, such as those in the 11 subsets coming out of the analyses. There are of course other ways of measuring these characteristics.

The hypotheses delineated here are of two types: research hypotheses and action hypotheses. These can readily be differentiated on the basis of the amount of statistical data supporting them. Generally speaking, all the hypotheses about motivation for work that make few, if any, assumptions about development are *action* hypotheses — that is, those that can be applied in a practical operating situation as if they were true. Those that assume some kind of developmental progression are *research* hypotheses that will ultimately require quite different research designs for their testing. In the final analysis, longitudinal studies will have to be done in order to determine how the work motivation of employed adults can be developed.

One set of general specifications can be cited of the dimensions on which a work-motivated adult can be described. Within the framework of all these results man can be described along seven basic dimensions:

1. His characteristic level of activation.
2. The extent to which his energy, at whatever level, is directed.
3. The extent to which he views work as a medium in which to exercise his social, intellectual, perceptual, and motor skills.
4. The extent to which he views work as a medium in which to acquire responsibility over other people and their activities.
5. The extent to which he views work as an instrumentality by means of which he can be liked or accepted by others or acquire security, wealth, or prestige.
6. The extent to which work and the conditions that surround it are threatening and generate anxiety and apprehensive behavior and attitudes.
7. The extent to which work and the conditions that surround it are irritating and generate pugnacious and aggressive behavior and attitudes.

BIOLOGICAL SECOND-LEVEL HYPOTHESES

From first exposure to Herzberg's data to the time when the exhibits shown in Chapter 2 emerged from a set of statistical operations, one difficulty recurred: These data would not integrate with a set of biological and psychological biases acquired through years of study and practice.

To the nonpsychologist this may not appear to be much of a problem, but since the theory that follows bears directly on its solution, it may be worthwhile to spell out some of its ramifications.

First, the feelings reported by Herzberg's interviewees fitted no known classification scheme in psychological science, even though they made sense in the light of personal experience. Psychology has long dealt with the basic emotions of love and hate and has studied their physiological concomitants, but what was to be made of feelings like responsibility or accomplishment? What are verbal responses? Are they mere sounds — noise accompanying behavior? Can they be treated as basic data, construed in terms of intended meanings? The nonpsychologist may have no trouble with these questions. But a psychologist, steeped in the tradition of behaviorism with its very good reasons for distrusting verbal communications, cannot readily answer them.

A second problem arises from the fact that, as reported, these feelings occurred *subsequent* to a job condition producing satisfaction and accompanied *augmented* work activity. Hence they cannot be accounted for by a need- or tension-reduction theory of motivation. This excludes the traditional physiological and the psychoanalytic theories of motivation as explanatory models.

A third well-known fact, not directly related to these data, was bothersome then as well as now because current theories of motivation could not explain it. The curve indicating the rate of acquisition of knowledge by man has been an accelerating one for several decades and a rapidly accelerating one since World War II. Assuming that no real change has occurred in the original nature of man over this brief period, how does one go about explaining this acceleration?

Other phenomena are notable in connection with this *knowledge explosion.* One is the population explosion — the increase in the number of people living in this finite space. Another is urbanization — the tendency of more and more people to occupy circumscribed city and metropolitan areas. A third is the rapid development of transportation and communication facilities, especially communication involving more of the senses and thus more immediate interpersonal contact. A higher standard of living, much more leisure time, and a safer, more secure environment may be added to these phenomena, at least in some cultures. These trends have produced a much larger population of men and women in direct and immediate contact with one another. Such trends may be the determinants for a period of intellectual progress that transcends any other in recorded history.

A Biological Bias

The science of zoology describes and classifies an animal according to a number of morphological dimensions and uses them as a basis for comparisons of animals across species, genera, classes, orders, and so forth. Organic systems — for example, the skeletal system and the circulatory system — have specific functions in support of the individual animal. The nervous system is described as the handmaiden or servant of the other systems, since in the higher mammals — for example, man — it is viewed as the mediator of their activities. All these systems have the same basic function: to support and maintain the animal until such time as it can reproduce itself, thus assuring the continuity of the species. The associated biological science, physiology, although concerned with the study of function rather than form, nevertheless appears to approach the study of animals from this same point of view.

Most theories of animal motivation are of the need- or tension-reduction type. In other words, activity is perceived to arise with the occurrence of a tension state and is continued until such time as the tension is reduced. One assumes the presence of a set of physiological needs that periodically recur and are satisfied by specific forms of activity designed to take care of them. Thirst and hunger are examples of physiological imbalances that generate activity until such time as a steady state returns. The function of the nervous system is considered to be one of mediating the activity required to resolve the imbalance.

In looking at such tension-reduction systems in man, several things are seen to be of particular significance. The physiological imbalance is accompanied by specific feelings, such as hunger and thirst. These feelings are commonly interpreted as evidence of the imbalance and generally accompany activity designed to reduce them. In extreme form, these feelings are unpleasant. They precede reward — for example, food — and disappear when the imbalance is alleviated or a homeostatic condition is reinstated. Their absence from consciousness is evidence of homeostasis.

The tensions produced by threatening or irritating stimuli are of essentially the same type. Anger and fear signify states of emotional tension in a person that disappear from consciousness when the irritating and threatening stimuli are removed. Not only does the feeling disappear, but so does the activity designed to reduce the tension. Anger and fear differ from hunger and thirst along a number of dimensions but are alike in the sense that they denote an imbalance and disappear when the imbalance has been resolved.

Both types of imbalance are compelling in the sense that they tend to generate behavior that supplants any other form of activity in which the person is engaged. Either type of imbalance, if sufficiently severe, can take precedence over the other. A thoroughly frightened animal may still seek food in a dangerous environment if sufficiently hungry. An extremely hungry animal may take time out to attack a natural enemy. A frightened animal has little time to do anything but try to escape a threatening environment. A hungry animal or hungry man has little time to do anything but seek food.

A frightened or hungry man may resort to *work* to reduce either tension state. But he works as a means to an end, not because he enjoys it, and will stop working when the tension state is resolved. The stimuli that generate physiological and emotional tensions do not generate pleasurable feelings and are not things that man seeks out deliberately.

An Alternative Bias

A tension-reduction theory of motivation obviously is consistent with the concept of the nervous system just outlined. Unfortunately, such a theory cannot account for the data collected by Herzberg. The temporal order of the reinforcement preceding the feeling precludes this. The fact that a reinforcing job condition maintains or augments activity rather than eliminating it is also incompatible with such a theory.

In line with common scientific practice, let us entertain an alternative way of looking at the nervous system and see where it leads us. This alternative is simply that the central nervous system, specifically the higher brain centers, is *an entity in its own right* and the other systems in the body — the muscular system, the circulatory system, and the rest — are its servants and aid and abet its need for survival.

Only one basic assumption needs to be made about this entity: Its maintenance and development depend on the extent to which it receives stimulation. This stimulation may be mediated by the senses or its own storage; that is, ideas and memories. A sizable body of neurophysiological evidence on the effects of sensory deprivation supports this view. For example, see the recent work by D. P. Schultz.[1]

[1]*Sensory Restriction: Effects on Behavior*, Academic Press, New York, 1965.

The Significance of Closure

A great mass of evidence supports Gestalt theory — the theory that describes the marked tendency for man to perceive and learn organized patterns of stimuli rather than disjointed elements — but there is little explanation of how or why this happens.

As indicated earlier, both in Herzberg's data and in the data reported here a frequently reported agent for reinforcing accomplishment motivation is the successful completion of a task. This is of course nothing but a special case of closure — the organization of a complex perceptual field or a complex set of motor activities into a unitary pattern. Man seeks closure at ever-increasing levels of complexity and directs his activities toward its accomplishment. It is reasonable to suggest that closure seeking is a natural function of this entity and serves to increase the stimulation potential of its psychological environment. The practicing of specific motor, perceptual, intellectual, and social skills is a form of self-stimulation leading, hopefully, to closure and hence to augmented satisfaction. Since work involves the exercise of one's skills, it can be stimulating in its own right or can represent an instrumentality through which stimulation can be obtained in some other way.

The differential patterning of interests and values describes the range of individual differences in the stimulation-seeking activity of men and women. By the same token, the differential patterning of skills and aptitudes describes the range of individual differences in the closure potential of men and women. The former yields information on what a man *will* do; the latter, on what a man *can* do, or will be able to do.

A Hierarchical Interpretation of Motivation

There appears to be validity to some concept of a hierarchy of needs of the type proposed by A. H. Maslow.[2] Three need systems, arranged in a hierarchy, are posited here, with the higher ones taking over when the lower ones are in a steady state. The lowest is the physiological drive system. Activity is generated in the organism whenever a specific physiological need — for example, food — throws the system out of balance, and this activity disappears when a balance has been restored. The second level is represented by an emotional drive system, which functions when

[2]"A Theory of Motivation," *Psychological Review,* Vol. 50: 1943, pp. 370-396.

the organism is threatened or irritated. Specific forms of activity are generated in the organism whenever emotional tension creates a sufficient
imbalance to induce activity. With the return of the tension to an acceptable level, this activity ceases. The third level may be appropriately labeled
an intellectual drive system. This is the only one of the three that does
not function as a homeostatic system, in the sense that reinforcement
deactivates the organism. Food-seeking behavior disappears when hunger
is sated. Aggressive behavior disappears when the irritant producing
it is eliminated. Stimulation-seeking behavior appears to continue indefi-
nitely and is not readily sated.

Maslow's concept of self-actualization is congruent with our alternative assumption about the nervous system. A self-actualized person might
be described as one who has realized the stimulation potential of *his*
environment.

Self-actualization cannot be achieved unless the two lower systems
are maintained as homeostatic systems with relatively little expenditure
of energy. Let us assume that there are individual differences in man's
characteristic level of activation. If the energy represented by the level
is directed toward resolving physiological or emotional disequilibria, little
is left over for exploring the stimulation potential of the psychological
environment. The circumscribed behavior that is adaptive in reducing
physiological and emotional tensions further restricts the reinforcement
potential of the total life space.

Continuing frustration — that is, the long-term inability of an environment to furnish stimulation or to reinforce the stimulation needs of a person
— may result in the destruction of his intellectual drive and turn him into
an animal or a vegetable. These latter two terms, in common language,
are apt descriptions of a man who characteristically responds emotionally
to his environment or spends his time responding to his physiological
needs. The evidence suggests strongly that alterations in the central nervous system produced by sensory deprivation can impair the ability to
organize, pattern, or restructure the psychological field. The effects of
sensory deprivation may show up at a very early age and produce impair-
ment that is retained throughout life.

A Systems Interpretation of the Central Nervous System

Since we are identifying the nervous system with the entity often
called the self, a useful purpose can be served by analyzing this entity

as a system and examining the implications of such a description. Broadly speaking, the functions of the nervous system are (1) input, (2) storage, (3) storage retrieval, (4) processing, (5) output. *Input* is talked about as sensing, perceiving, or feeling; *storage*, as learning or memorizing; *storage retrieval*, as recalling; *processing*, as judging, thinking, or reasoning; and *output*, as behaving or reporting.

One additional assumption will be made about the nervous system: *All* inputs are stored, but not necessarily in a form that will permit ready retrieval. Inputs may be stored without processing and without initiating an output. Stored inputs may be retrieved and initiate an output; they may be retrieved, processed, and returned to storage with or without initiating an output. It is apparent that the functions labeled input, storage, storage retrieval, and processing can go on without involving the output function; that is, without generating behavior. Storage retrieval and processing can go on without involving either the input or output functions of the system. Not only *can* they go on, but most of this activity *does* go on without being initiated by a specific sensory input and without a behavioral resultant.

The Biological Function of Behavior

The assumption of a need for stimulation is sufficient to account for any of these functions that do not involve an output. What useful purposes, then, are served by the output components of this system? Two are immediately obvious. The glandular and motor behaviors mediated by the autonomic nervous system serve the adaptive functions of maintaining the organism as a physiological system and preparing it for violent activity. Specific efferent or output components of the central nervous system aid and abet these two functions. However, most of the activities mediated by the output component of the central nervous system are not related to either of these two. The question remains: What functions do they serve? They seem to serve three.

First, activity per se is a direct source of stimulation — by way of the kinesthetic feedback mechanism, for example. Second, activity positions the individual with respect to his stimulus field in such a way as to furnish a different set of inputs into the system. This permits an enrichment of the stimulus field. Third, activity permits communication with or stimulation of a second individual.

This third function needs some elaboration. It seems reasonable to ascribe to language (verbal behavior) the primary biological function of enriching the sensory inputs of *other* nervous systems. Each person has available, to a greater or lesser degree, a device by which the activity of his nervous system can be made known to others and thus incorporated in their own. Any form of communication — be it language, art, music, or drama — is a device for transmitting the stored contents of one nervous system to another. Obviously, the more people in communication with one another, the greater the stimulation for all.

The Knowledge Explosion

This extension of motivation theory, especially as it refers to the stimulation value of communication, provides the link needed to account for the knowledge explosion.

In the past few decades man has lived in an environment requiring a diminishing expenditure of energy in reducing physiological and emotional tension, thus freeing the energy for closure seeking. Thanks to the population explosion, increasing urbanization, and rapid technological advances in transportation and communications media, many more people are now in direct and immediate communication with one another, thus enriching the stimulation potential of each person's social environment. The combination of these factors has permitted man to function much closer to his intellectual capacity. His energy has been channeled into activities that have been both satisfying (rewarding) to him and beneficial to society in general.

The knowledge explosion has been produced primarily by *employed* men and women. A great many people are rediscovering daily that their own stimulation needs are most readily and efficiently satisfied by the infinite variety of interesting and challenging activities to be found in the world of work.

* * *

This chapter has attempted to organize the results of the research into a set of hypotheses about motivation for work. They are descriptive hypotheses in the sense that they indicate either how work-motivated people view work or what work-motivated people are like as people. Both of these "aspects" of work motivation can be described by simple, generalized systems.

The chapter also has attempted to answer the "why" of human motivation by recourse to a few well-documented neurophysiological facts, one general assumption about the need of man for intellectual stimulation, and a consideration of the role of behavior in satisfying that stimulation need. This led to a theory of adult motivation simple in outline, but with ramifications extending beyond the scope of this book.

The descriptive hypotheses are of two types: (1) Those that are suggested by the data, but not well supported by statistical evidence, are in the nature of research hypotheses — that is, their presentation is meant to stimulate further research by others or to specify the direction of PSP's research efforts. (2) Those hypotheses that are well supported by the statistical evidence presented here are in the nature of action hypotheses — that is, they are documented well enough to suggest that in an operational setting they can be acted on as if they were true. These latter hypotheses, then, have practical implications for the selection, development, and management of people in industrial settings, as discussed in the following chapter.

9

Practical Implications

THE MATERIAL IN CHAPTERS 2 TO 7 and its summarization in Chapter 8 indicate that the results reported have many practical implications for the selection, management, and development of people at work. Many of these implications were either stated or implied in the earlier chapters, and the purpose of this chapter is to organize them into a coherent framework. Before doing that, however, let us take a closer look at several aspects of the measurement problem in relation to motivation for work and discuss the significance of the drive characteristic isolated in the research.

The Measurement Problem

In the study reported on here, information on motivation and its measurement was obtained by asking a person how he responded to his job (the Hackman Job Satisfaction Schedule) or how he typically behaved, responded to, or felt about a variety of life experiences (the Guilford-Zimmerman Temperament Survey). The assumption was that *the way a man perceives himself is the way he is.* In using the Thematic Apperception Test, D. C. McClelland in *The Achievement Motive*[1] operated on the assumption that *the way a man projects himself into, or interprets, an ambiguous situation is the way he is.*

There are other ways in which information about motivation can be obtained. A third way is to attend to personal history information—the objective record of what a person has done at school, at work, at home, and in society. In using this kind of information it would have to be assumed that what an individual has done in the past he will continue to do; *what he was in the past, he is in the present and will be in the future.*

The fourth way would be to ask people who know a man well to evaluate him on the motivational characteristics identified in the factor analyses or those defined by the 11 motivation subscales. In using this procedure, it would have to be assumed that *the way a man is perceived by others is the way he is.*

Undoubtedly, there is a certain amount of truth in all these assumptions. The choice of a measuring system on the basis of any one in preference to the others depends on the predilections of the information gatherer and the practical problem of measuring a particular factor in a given operating situation. However, since the data reported on in this book are based on the first assumption, the others will require research to determine the conditions for their optimal use.

THE DRIVE CHARACTERISTIC

Ordinarily when we speak of a man as having a lot of drive we are suggesting two things. First, we are saying that he invests his activity with a good deal of energy or "push"; that is, the *quantum* aspect. Second, we are implying that his strivings are organized with reference to some aim; that is, the *directional* aspect. Direction and intensity always appear together in motivated behavior, which is why motives are often viewed as vectors by motivation theorists.

We are likely to distinguish between these two aspects in practice. For example, we see two men pursuing the same general goal, but one pursues it actively, vigorously, and with all the resources at his command; the other does so desultorily, sporadically, and without vigor. We say that the first man has a lot of drive whereas the second, however high his aspirations, lacks push. The two differ in the quantum aspect. Men

[1]Appleton-Century-Crofts, New York, 1953.

also differ in the directional aspect: Two men may be quite similar in sheer vitality or energy level, but one marshals his energies persistently and effectively in pursuit of his goals, while the other dissipates his in varied pursuits, distractions, and generally unorganized activity.

As has been pointed out, the drive characteristic appeared as a distinct aspect of three of the four HJSS motivation factors: A, B, and N. Let us consider some of the general interpretative features of the three motivation scales describing it.

The B_1 scale describes a person's perception of how energetically he works in comparison with others. His energy is *work directed; that is,* tied to work activities (direction). A person showing a high score on the B_1 scale is also saying that he invests a great deal of energy in work (quantum). It may be recalled that high B_1 scores were generally characteristic of the salaried groups and differentiated effectively between high and low performers in those groups.

The A_1 scale describes a person's perception of his available energy, apart from work but not necessarily divorced from it. A person scoring high on A_1 is saying, in effect, that he has a lot of vitality, but he is communicating this through the medium of a set of items that have no reference to work activities. Its linkage with the accomplishment factor suggests that a high A_1 score characterizes a man who energetically pursues activities to further his own personal stimulation seeking, whether or not these are related to work. Further research will reveal whether A_1 is high, as expected, in the individualistically creative occupations such as art, writing, drama, and scientific research and whether this is at the expense of B_1. The significance of this characteristic for performance was ambiguous in the industrial groups.

The N_1 scale is, to a large extent, the negative of B_1. A person scoring high on N_1 is saying he lacks energy and is spiritless and inactive. What kind of person is likely to describe himself in this way? To begin with he may be genuinely lacking in vitality—that is, lethargic—and perceive himself as such. The high N_1 signifies little quantum—a lazy person. Or such a person may be describing himself in this way because he is chronically blocked as a result of oppressive circumstances (lack of opportunity, for example, or indecisive vocational objectives) or internal difficulties (such as anxiety or inner conflict). In the latter case, the high N_1 signifies a lack of outlet, a blocked person.

So much for the individual scales. In practice the three scales occur in combinations, and the meaning that can be assigned to any one grouping depends on the interrelations among the three. Since B_1 and N_1 are necessarily negatively correlated, because some items are common to both but scored in opposite directions, instances of high B_1 combined with high N_1 or low B_1 with low N_1 cannot occur. Let us consider a few of the possible combinations.

High B_1 / high A_1 / low N_1. This pattern bespeaks a high level of work-directed energy with high energy reserves for activities other than work. It describes a person who can and does work vigorously at his job all day every day and still has the energy to pursue family, social, and other activities.

High B_1/low A_1/low N_1. This pattern describes a high level of energy focused exclusively on work and work-related activities.

Low B_1 / high A_1 / high N_1. This pattern describes a person who is energetic in pursuing things that interest him but is unable to meet work demands consistently or with comparable vigor. In the samples this pattern was frequent among younger college students. Thus it may characterize the person of good energy resources who has not as yet made a satisfying work commitment. Since this pattern also occurs in hourly workers it may have similar significance there.

Low B_1/ low A_1/ high N_1. This pattern suggests a lack of energy and vitality. The person is describing himself as unable to pursue any form of satisfying activity. We would expect to find such a person either lethargic or blocked.

High A_1/ moderate to low B_1/ moderate to low N_1. Since A_1 dominates this pattern, it depicts a person of good energy resources who will work when it suits him at activities that interest him. He is not inclined to make much accommodation to external demands, and his dedication to work may therefore be somewhat sporadic or inconsistent.

IMPLICATIONS FOR SELECTION

The validity data reported in Chapter 7 suggest that most motivational characteristics have some value for selection, either because different jobs require different degrees of various characteristics or because people with these characteristics in whatever degree will find some kinds of work rewarding and not others. Before taking up the implications of specific characteristics, however, let us consider a few general aspects of the selection problem.

All selection procedures run the risk of overselection; and overselection with respect to motivational characteristics may have even more damaging repercussions than overselection with respect to ability or skill. This may be because ability and skill are more peripheral and variable in relation to temperament than is motivation. For example, if we overselect young women for secretarial work by hiring many whose abilities exceed the demands of the job, we may lose some who find the work uninteresting; but many will remain because, whatever their abilities, their temperaments do not demand or perhaps even desire challenging work.

In selecting on the basis of motivational characteristics, however, we are moving close to the heart of what makes work rewarding or frustrating. Here overselection can be expected to result in higher attrition rates as those who are highly motivated do not find their needs fulfilled, in increased discontent as those who remain become dissatisfied, and in the active sharing of this discontent with others. If overselection has been the rule rather than the exception, it is obvious that those who remain will find others of like mind, and situations will develop for the formation of negative group attitudes.

The availability of a system for defining and measuring motivational characteristics associated with work adds a new and potentially valuable dimension to selection. However, its use implies the acquisition of specific information about another dimension of work: the reinforcement potential of a given job and the job hierarchy in which it is embedded. This probably means the development of a new set of job analysis and job description procedures.

In addition to work on job definition from a motivational standpoint, the nature of the relationships between specific motivational characteristics and job performance deserves careful attention. These relationships may at times be curvilinear rather than rectilinear. In other words, the possession of a given characteristic may be positively related to performance *up to a certain level* but may become increasingly nonadaptive, if not maladaptive, beyond this level. Consider, for example, the accomplishment drive or need for closure. Men with strong motivation of this kind may find the ambiguity and absence of closure that characterize the work of top management not only distasteful but actually demoralizing.

Finally, selection is rarely looked upon as just a matter of deciding a person's fitness for a specific job. It is also a matter of estimating his potential for development and change and of projecting this growth potential to a hierarchy of jobs of which the specific one is but a first step. Thus the selection specialist must take an interest in the dynamic features of the applicant's characteristics (skills, abilities, motivations) as a basis for selection. (In the language of the psychologist, the selection specialist must be concerned with an applicant's susceptibility to differentiation and change with time and experience and the effectiveness of procedures for exploiting these susceptibilities.) The selection manager faces a necessary dilemma here: Although he must select for potential, he must also recognize that overselection for a particular job risks the loss of a man because of an initial lack of reinforcement. A person may, with good grace, temporarily forgo the exercise of certain skills if he can see prospects for using them in the future, but it is difficult for him to function for long in an unstimulating or nonreinforcing work environment. The developmental question therefore cannot be divorced from the problem of selection.

The Work-Directed Drive Characteristic

Work-directed drive is indicated by the extent to which a person perceives how energetically and efficiently he works in comparison to others. This kind of channeled or harnessed energy is positively correlated with success on most jobs, although the energy level requirement varies from job to job. It is more characteristic of salaried employees than of hourly employees and is more characteristic of managers than of salaried employees who do not have managerial responsibility. Evidence of this characteristic can be obtained from many sources besides the one used here; it is readily observed in others and easily evaluated.

The energy classified by the A_1 scale characterizes a person who would be deemed hyperactive — a man who turns his energy on and off at will, who pursues activities that further his own personal stimulation seeking even though they may be quite tangential to his work. It goes along with closure seeking, the accomplishment-oriented drive, and is characteristic of people who are likely to be threatened or irritated by their jobs. Men with this type of energy will work, but just when and how is difficult to predict.

Of peculiar significance to the selection of people for different kinds of jobs are combinations of the work-directed and hyperactive characteristics. A man can show both highly developed, or neither, or one but not the other. The person who exhibits both works effectively all day, every day of the week, and actively pursues family, social, civic, and sports activities during nonwork hours. The man with neither type well developed will exhibit a low energy level at work and away from work. The man with a high level of work-directed energy and little of the free-floating type cannot be enticed into the pursuit of activities that do not have immediately obvious significance for work. The man with a great deal of free-floating energy but little directed energy will work when it suits him at activities that interest him. Whether these activities are congruent with a company's goals is of minor concern to him.

From the point of view of efficient selection, one puts the first of these men in a job that will tax his energy and pays him enough to permit him to indulge his off-the-job interests. One puts the second man in a job that is neither particularly demanding nor critical to the overall success of the company. The third man can be put on a demanding job, but not one requiring effort tangential to the work itself. The fourth man is going to work when and as he pleases. He should not be put in a job requiring continuous attention to administrative detail, nor should he be expected to produce in the prescribed workday.

The Emotional-Tension Factors

The evidence on the validity of measures of anxiety and aggression in predicting job performance is reasonably clear-cut. People who show either or both traits to a high degree are poor risks for employment. These characteristics can be tolerated in women more than in men and in hourly paid workers more than in salaried workers. However, the extent of the tolerance has to be determined for specific jobs and specific work situations.

There is a strong suggestion in the data that people who can "take things in stride" — that is, who are not readily irritated or threatened — tend to perform well in jobs that are people-tied. For example, they perform well in jobs that require extensive interaction with people in the salesmen-customer or supervisor-subordinate relationship. The implications for selection are obvious.

We should note that the responsibility seeker is as a rule a relatively calm person. Many accomplishment-oriented people, on the other hand, exhibit this emotional-tension characteristic to a marked degree.

The Motivation Channels

The remaining three of the seven dimensions along which motivation for work can be described are qualitatively different, since they are concerned with the way in which a man views work as a source of satisfaction, and they fit a system that has implications for selection. The first two, closure seeking and responsibility seeking, characterize men who view work as a direct means by which their motivations can be satisfied. The third, an instrumentalist pattern, characterizes men who view work as a means to some other end, such as money, security, or prestige. The first two signify independent but not incompatible patterns, since closure seeking and responsibility seeking can be satisfied within the framework of the same job. Frequently, however, they are not satisfied because the role of the supervisor or the manager is to arrange for *others* to exercise their specialized technical skills rather than to exercise their own. Therefore, closure must be experienced vicariously, not directly.

Closure seekers can be identified by characteristics other than hyperactivity and egocentricity — the two isolated in this study. These men have been trained in or have developed specialized competence in skill areas with which they are personally identified. For example, if they have been trained as chemical engineers, they expect to work on chemical engineering problems and feel that nothing else is quite so important. They are typically task-oriented and concentrate or dissipate their energies to suit themselves. They identify themselves as chemical engineers and expect to retain this identification throughout their careers.

Responsibility seekers, on the other hand, even though they also may have been trained as engineers, perceive their training as preparation for supervision and management. Their engineering skills are viewed as subordinate to the interpersonal skills they use in organizing and directing the work of others. They do not apply themselves to becoming better engineers; their focus is on becoming better managers. They prefer that specialized skills be represented in their subordinates and are happy to see these skills exercised. They will assume responsibility for duties other than engineering and will work at them with equal energy. They budget their energies in order to distribute them effectively.

Closure seekers are likely to judge the returns on their training investments in terms of the size and importance of the problems they work on. They may move to another company if its problems are perceived as more interesting and challenging. In contrast, responsibility seekers judge the return on their training investments in terms of the size and complexity of the organizations they work in and may move to larger and more complex organizations to satisfy their needs for greater responsibility.

The third of these dimensions, the instrumentalist pattern, has been described as an extrinsic channel. People with this kind of motivation view work as a means to an end; they work for satisfactions not intrinsic to the activity itself. These people have been called instrumentalists because the scales derived from the G-ZTS classify them as manipulators of people and social situations. Viewed in this fashion, this kind of motivation does not seem to typify the hourly worker in industry. He is a means-end person in a sense, but his substitute satisfactions are of an order different from those of salaried personnel. The data presented in Chapters 5 and 6 suggest that since most hourly workers would deny having this characteristic, it should be used as a negative predictor rather than a positive one in the selection of hourly people. This assumes that hourly work offers few rewards and little satisfaction for men motivated in this fashion; hence they are likely to move on to greener pastures.

Certain other groups of employees have this kind of extrinsic motivation; for example, the industrial salesmen used in the research and, in particular, the securities salesmen. A somewhat surprising finding was that although this type of motivation was not very highly developed in research and development managers, its absence related to poor performance. Also noteworthy is that the women in the sample denied that they had either none or much of this motivation.

This motivational characteristic is exceedingly complex, and this research does little to define it. Interestingly, the reinforcing agents on the job form a homogeneous set — a promotion, a raise, and increased status. The heterogeneity is represented in the feelings generated by any of these agents. The one thing that instrumentalists have in common is their view of work as a means to some other end. That end or goal may be social acceptance, security, prestige, money, or whatever money may represent. One characteristic of these people seems to be that they are generalists rather than specialists and are likely to be highly trained in a skill area.

IMPLICATIONS FOR THE MANAGEMENT OF MEN

Along with the problem of selecting men appropriately motivated for the jobs in a company is the associated problem of arranging so that each man's motivation is appropriately reinforced. Management has two concerns here. The first is a hard-headed concern — unless a motivated employee is suitably rewarded for his efforts, his production will fall off, with a corresponding cost to the company. The second concern is that unless a motivated employee is appropriately rewarded for his efforts he will become unhappy with his lot, exhibit low morale, and probably try to promote dissatisfaction in other people. Presumably, the goal of management is twofold: (1) production with (2) accompanying employee satisfaction.

The data presented in this book make it clear that people are complicated, motivationally speaking, at whatever level they operate in the industrial hierarchy. Not everyone is likely to be motivated in the same way, and the projection of one's own motivation into another is both an unrewarding and a dangerous pastime — unrewarding because it will probably serve no useful function in directing the activities of a second person and dangerous because it may generate emotional tension rather than reinforce motivation.

Any supervisor or manager has a dual responsibility in this connection. First, he needs to acquire information on the motivational systems of the men under his management; he must learn to know them as individuals. Second, he must try to adapt the available reinforcing agents to the range of individual differences among the men he has working for him. One man may need to be praised irrespective of what he does; a second should be praised selectively; a third should be listened to but not praised. One may need to have minor responsibilities placed on his shoulders endlessly; a second may need to be free of the burden altogether.

Herzberg found that one of the frequently reported feelings accompanying dissatisfaction was that of being treated unfairly. The same was seen in PSP's survey data. This could be interpreted to mean that everyone should be treated the same — which might be valid if all people were the same. However, what is interpreted as fair by one man is interpreted as unfair by another. Being treated fairly is a matter of being treated as an individual, with all the *differential* treatment this implies. You are not being fair to a closure seeker if you do not permit him to exercise his skills. You are not being fair to a responsibility seeker if you do not give him people to supervise.

A first-line supervisor has to be a responsibility seeker, since he is a reinforcing agent in the work environment. He must operate without positive feedback. Both the data reported here and Herzberg's data strongly suggest that a supervisor is viewed as a source of satisfaction only when he does not obviously supervise. Rarely are supervisors cited as sources of satisfaction. Perhaps the only time he is likely to hear from his subordinates that he is doing a good job is when his management elects to do an attitude survey. On the other hand, supervision is a powerful source of dissatisfaction in subordinates. Witness the frequent mention of critical, unfriendly, and incompetent supervision and poor organization of work as sources of dissatisfaction.

There are relatively few things an immediate supervisor can do to reinforce the motivation of his men. For those whose motivation is essentially that of closure seeking, he can (1) arrange to give them jobs that are challenging but within the limits of their capabilities; (2) exercise permissive supervision and let them do the job in their own way; and (3) give them positive feedback — praise — for work accomplished. For the responsibility seekers among his subordinates, he can arrange to give them supervisory and training responsibility for the work of others; he can in a sense lend them some of his own responsibility for the work of the unit he supervises.

The reinforcement of those with means-end orientations toward work appears to be the province of higher management, not of the immediate supervisors. The *authority* for pay raises and promotions is ordinarily not vested in immediate supervision. Management decides whether a person will have a secretary, a private parking space, a two-pedestal rather than a one-pedestal desk. It also decides whether work units will be organized into four-, eight-, or sixteen-man units; whether shifts will be retained intact or placed on multiple schedules; whether individuals or groups will be rewarded for money-saving suggestions. How often does management know its men well enough to distribute such reinforcements meaningfully?

So far the implications of the positive motivational characteristics in the management of men has been considered. The scales and factors describing the ways in which men are threatened or irritated by their jobs are also significant. Responding frequently in either of these ways is nonadaptive in most people in most jobs, probably because the resulting behavior and attitudes are not congruent with the work activity itself.

There is no doubt that many people can be activated by anxiety. Some managers and some personnel men honestly believe that the only way to get a man to work is to frighten him or to make him angry. However, anger and anxiety are not the only negative feelings that are generated by threatening and irritating stimuli.

Mention was made previously of an inability to detect in the Herzberg data a pattern of relationships among feeling states and job conditions for the unhappy episodes. It also was pointed out that a somewhat different set of job conditions and feelings was used by Herzberg's interviewees in describing these unhappy episodes. It was because of this that the negative sets of conditions and feelings used in the attitude survey contained items not represented in the two positive sets. (These items are listed in Appendix B.)

In 1962 an intercorrelation matrix was factored describing the interrelationships among the 13 negative feelings and 14 job conditions. This matrix was calculated from data on one group of men who filled out the questionnaire as part of the attitude survey. Seven factors or patterns accounted for the intercorrelations among the items. These seven factors could be rotated to simple structure by means of oblique rotations, but most of the resulting combinations of job conditions and feelings made little psychological or common sense. A few clear-cut and readily anticipated combinations did emerge. For example, a report of not getting a raise and a promotion was accompanied by a feeling of not making financial progress.

Since this analysis did not appear to be fruitful, further attempts to work with these data were abandoned. In 1967, however, the thought occurred that, even though the intercorrelations among the elements in the complete set of feelings and job conditions could not be factored meaningfully, it might be possible to make some sense out of the intercorrelations among the feeling words alone. The end product of the ensuing analysis follows.

Four clear-cut factors emerged. One is a *frustration-aggression* factor whose pattern comprises feelings of (1) things being unfair, (2) being blocked from growing and developing, (3) a lack of accomplishment, and (4) being just plain "mad." The second is an *anxiety* factor comprising feelings of (1) isolation, (2) insecurity, (3) inadequacy, and (4) anxiety. The third factor reflects *personal inadequacy*, combining feelings of (1) lack of accomplishment, (2) shame, (3) inadequacy, and (4) loss of confidence. The fourth factor is *social rejection*, encompassing feelings of (1) lack of recognition, (2) isolation, (3) insecurity, (4) loss of confidence, and (5) rejection.

To summarize, these men are reporting that events and conditions at work (1) frustrated them and made them angry, (2) made them anxious, (3) made them feel personally inadequate, and (4) made them feel socially rejected. The major question, of course, is, "What conditions and events produced these feelings?"

An answer was obtained by resorting to a supplementary analysis. The conditions that produced each of the feeling patterns was identified by noting conditions that correlated consistently and with some magnitude with all the feeling words in each pattern. Exhibit 47 identifies the conditions associated with each pattern. In this exhibit the number of X's indicates, roughly, the relative strength of the association.

Several things are immediately apparent from this exhibit. First, many different conditions can produce each of the negative feeling patterns. Second, certain conditions apparently can produce them all; for example, no praise, poor organization of work, and critical, unfriendly, and incompetent supervision. Third, a few conditions are quite specifically tied to certain feeling patterns. No promotion is correlated only with the social rejection pattern; failure in a task results only in a feeling of anxiety or personal inadequacy; loss of face leads only to a feeling of anxiety or social rejection. Fourth, two conditions do not generate any of

EXHIBIT 47

**Relationships Between Specific Sources of
Dissatisfaction and Feeling Patterns
Accompanying Them**

| | Negative Feeling Pattern | | | |
Source of Dissatisfaction	Frustration-Aggression	Anxiety	Personal Inadequacy	Social Rejection
No promotion				X
No raise	X		X	X
Loss of face		XX		XX
Dull work	XX		X	X
Failure to complete a task		X	X	
No praise	XX	XXX	XX	XXX
Close supervision	XX		X	X
Critical supervision	X	XX	X	X
Unfriendly supervision	XX	XX	X	XX
Incompetent supervision	XX	XXX	X	XX
Poor organization of work	XXX	XXX	XXX	XXX
Poor personnel policies	XX	X		XX
Disagreement with company goals	X	X		X
Poor relations with subordinates				
Poor work by subordinates				

these feelings: poor work by subordinates and poor relations with subordinates.

The groupings under the sources of dissatisfaction correspond to their positive counterparts that serve to reinforce the instrumentalist, the closure seeker, and the responsibility seeker. Many of these conditions, of course, have no positive counterpart. One general conclusion can be drawn from this grouping: Different patterns of relationships characterize the positive and negative data. The absence of a reinforcing agent does not have the same significance as its presence. Any one irritant or threatening condition can and does generate quite different responses in different people and varied responses in the same person at various times.

One cannot help but be impressed by the widespread effect of supervision in producing these unpleasant feeling states. Two points stand out regarding the negative role a supervisor can play. First, he can deliberately withhold reinforcement by not rewarding motivated men. Second, he can generate dissatisfaction that will probably interfere with a man's activity.

There are a few things that a supervisor can be or do that are *guaranteed* to produce dissatisfaction and accompanying emotional tension. He can be incompetent, can organize work poorly for his men, can withhold praise, or can be critical and unfriendly. Whether these things produce anger, anxiety, feelings of inadequacy, or feelings of social rejection depends on the particular person being subjected to these kinds of treatment.

IMPLICATIONS FOR DEVELOPMENT

In Chapter 8 a set of hypotheses was presented about developmental progressions in two of the three motivational channels. The suggestion was made there that, in the case of accomplishment motivation, reporting feelings of recognition, confidence, or accomplishment signified a man's level of maturity. These words probably also indicate the extent to which a man's present skill level satisfies his expectations regarding his skill potential.

In the data recognition was most frequently linked with praise, confidence with successful completion of a task and permissive supervision, and accomplishment with interesting and challenging work. Seemingly, in order to develop this kind of motivation one arranges for the higher-level reinforcements or rewards to operate.

However, since this type of motivation is tied to the exercise of specific skills, reinforcing this kind of motivation is ineffective unless the man is also given the opportunity both to sharpen his present skills and to develop new ones. If skill *training* is not made available to a man at work, he will develop skills to be exercised outside of work and may end up viewing work as a set of activities to be tolerated rather than a set to be enjoyed.

Training can and should be interpreted as a reinforcing agent. It should serve the useful function of increasing the closure potential of a man's work. It should be looked at by management as a motivating agent as well as a specific device to increase production. In attitude surveys, the lack of training opportunities is a frequently mentioned source of dissatisfaction. This may mean that the rank and file in a company view training as the responsibility of management in the same way that they view education as the responsibility of government.

Training is meaningless to a man with little accomplishment motivation or to a man permanently fixated on a given level in the hierarchy. To a person with relatively little natural talent it is less meaningful than to one more generously endowed. Its motivational impact will probably lessen as a man moves along in his career.

Chapter 8 posited two levels of what has been called responsibility-seeking motivation. Since being given supervision over others is the necessary condition for the reinforcement of this kind of motivation, obviously it cannot be developed in a man unless he is given an opportunity to oversee the work of others. How management goes about arranging for a person with this set of motivational attitudes to learn to derive satisfaction from the delegation of responsibility to others is another thing. The techniques used in development as contrasted to training may be the answer to the question of how to move a man from the responsibility level to the growth level.

One of the more serious problems faced in industry is that of preparing an individual for retirement. Many men in managerial jobs have difficulty accepting retirement and adjusting to it. The reason for this may well be a function of the kind of motivation they have. For a responsibility seeker, accustomed to reinforcement from his numerous responsibilities, the reassignment of these responsibilities to others leaves a void that is exceedingly difficult to fill. The usual procedure in industry is to gradually transfer his duties to others, in the hope that off-the-job responsibilities will fill the gap left in the job. Many men manage this quite well by assuming religious, political, educational, or civic responsibilities. For some men, off-the-job responsibilities may be particularly rewarding, since their scope is so broad.

It is difficult at the moment to see a developmental sequence in the third of the three channels identified in the research. The means-end factor is characterized by homogeneity among the reinforcing agents and heterogeneity among the feeling responses. A developmental sequence could be posited in this area, but at the present time this would amount to sheer speculation. How should social approval, security, money, and prestige be arranged in a developmental sequence? The problem has immediate research implications.

It is axiomatic that there cannot be progress unless there is change. The data presented in Chapter 5 on the test-retest reliability of the individual motivation scales does not offer much encouragement about the possibility of producing change; that is, developing motivation in people. It was shown in Exhibit 14 that no significant *average* shifts in scale scores occurred over a two- to six-year period. These data were based on 92 cases in which men were seen for psychological appraisal twice, with varying periods of time intervening between a first and a second self-description. Of course, it can be argued that no significant change in the motivational conditions under which these men were operating occurred during this time; hence we would not expect any significant change in their motivation.

An examination of PSP files located 22 cases on which the G-ZTS was administered twice. In each of these cases the first description was made by the person as a counseling case, the second as an appraisal case.

The two sets of self-descriptions were scored for the motivation scales detailed in Chapter 4. Exhibit 48 shows what happened to these scales between the first and second administrations of the G-ZTS. The exhibit gives the mean differences in scale scores between the appraisal condition and the counseling condition, the value of t for each difference, and an indication of the statistical significance of the difference.

It may be noted that at the time of the second administration these men described themselves as significantly more industrious (B_1), socially aggressive (B_2), friendly and tolerant (B_3), serious minded and confident (B_4), and sociable (C_1). They said they had essentially the same degree of assertiveness (C_2), hyperactivity (A_1), and egocentricity (A_2). They also described themselves as significantly less lethargic (N_1), less anxiety ridden (N_2), and less pugnacious and resentful (N_3). It cannot be ascertained whether these changes stem from the conditions under which they filled out the questionnaire (counseling versus appraisal),

EXHIBIT 48

Counseling-Appraisal Test-Retest
Motivation Scale Shifts — $N = 22$

	Mean Scale Score			Significance Level *
	Counseling	Appraisal		
B_1 — Industriousness	11.4	16.0	5.4	<.001
B_2 — Social aggressiveness	11.5	17.0	5.1	<.001
B_3 — Friendliness	12.9	15.2	2.5	<.05
B_4 — Serious mindedness	11.9	16.5	4.8	<.001
C_1 — Sociability	10.5	13.1	4.0	<.001
C_2 — Assertiveness	9.8	10.8	1.3	>.05
A_1 — Hyperactivity	9.2	9.6	.5	>.05
A_2 — Egocentricity	14.0	14.1	.05	>.05
N_1 — Spiritlessness	6.3	2.3	− 4.7	<.001
N_2 — Anxiety	26.5	18.7	− 4.1	<.001
N_3 — Aggression	16.5	10.4	− 3.9	<.001

*These values indicate the probabilities of the occurrence of such a shift under conditions of random sampling or chance.

a positive effect of counseling on their earlier difficulties, or motivational development over time. It is noteworthy, however, that at the time of the appraisal situation they indicated they had a higher directed energy level and were more responsibility-oriented, less anxiety ridden, and less aggressive. Their accomplishment drive and status drive showed fewer significant changes, except that the men appeared to be somewhat more sociable.

These data show that people describe their motivation differently at different times. Adaptive changes do occur, and it should be possible to discover how to make them occur.

Appendix A

Initial and Terminal Factor Patterns;
Attitude Survey Motivation Items;
Hourly Production and Maintenance Workers; $N = 109$

	Initial Pattern			Terminal Pattern			Communality
	C_1	C_2	C_3	T_1	T_2	T_3	
Events or Conditions							
Promotion	.79	− .36	.18	.63	.07	.63	.80
Permissive supervision	.91	.12	− .18	.89	.29	.11	.89
Interesting work	.73	.14	− .28	.72	.35	.01	.64
Supervision of others	.71	− .37	− .25	.53	.47	46	.71
Raise	.84	− .04	.07	.78	.09	.32	.72
Successful completion of a task	.77	.21	− .11	.79	.17	.01	.65
Praise	.64	.22	.22	.69	− .16	.08	.51
Increased status	.68	− .24	.27	.57	− .07	.52	.60
Work of subordinates	.88	− .31	.15	.73	.10	.60	.90
Feelings							
Accomplishment	.93	.18	− .07	.93	.17	.10	.90
Confidence	.82	.20	− .15	.83	.22	.03	.74
Recognition	.92	.10	.24	.91	− .10	.28	.92
Pride	.81	.19	.04	.83	.04	.10	.70
Security	.80	.18	.20	.82	− .11	.16	.71
Financial progress	.86	.04	.10	.83	.04	.27	.76
Personal growth	.82	.05	.10	.79	.03	.24	.68
Responsibility	.74	− .24	− .16	.61	.35	.39	.65
Importance	.83	− .05	.16	.77	.01	.36	.72
Acceptance	.50	.10	− .03	.50	.08	.06	.26
Percentage contribution to variance				80	06	14	

	Transformation Matrix		
	T_1	T_2	T_3
C_1	.94	.17	.31
C_2	.34	− .30	− .89
C_3	.05	− .94	.34

EXHIBIT A-2

Initial and Terminal Factor Patterns; Attitude Survey Motivation Items; Hourly Production Workers; $N = 135$

	Initial Pattern				Terminal Pattern				Communality
	C_1	C_2	C_3	C_4	T_1	T_2	T_3	T_4	
Events or Conditions									
Promotion	.33	.14	− .41	.31	.15	− .06	.58	.18	.39
Permissive supervision	.72	− .08	.16	.36	.52	.30	.21	.53	.68
Interesting work	.83	.08	.11	− .20	.84	.18	.09	.05	.75
Supervision of others	.56	− .18	− .37	.09	.34	.31	.52	.02	.48
Raise	.62	.13	− .34	.08	.49	.04	.52	.07	.52
Successful completion of a task	.78	.14	.25	.13	.73	.12	.07	.40	.71
Praise	.68	.25	− .19	.16	.58	− .05	.44	.22	.58
Increased status	.33	− .31	.34	.08	.24	.42	− .18	.25	.32
Work of subordinates	.46	− .25	.13	.35	.24	.38	.14	.43	.41
Feelings									
Accomplishment	.82	.31	.18	.10	.81	− .04	.14	.36	.81
Confidence	.91	.24	.11	− .13	.93	.05	.15	.15	.91
Recognition	.74	.12	.18	− .17	.78	.12	.02	.10	.63
Pride	.83	.17	.20	− .13	.86	.10	.04	.16	.78
Security	.76	.31	− .10	− .16	.79	− .07	.28	.01	.71
Financial progress	.78	− .13	.05	− .19	.72	.36	.13	.01	.67
Personal growth	.79	− .25	− .07	− .20	.68	.47	.23	− .06	.74
Responsibility	.64	− .34	− .20	− .11	.47	.50	.32	− .08	.58
Importance	.58	− .18	.10	− .23	.55	.35	.00	− .05	.43
Acceptance	.85	− .11	− .17	− .18	.74	.35	.35	− .06	.80
Percentage contribution to variance					66	12	14	08	

Transformation Matrix

	T_1	T_2	T_3	T_4
C_1	.88	.30	.31	.21
C_2	.28	− .95	.04	.09
C_3	.19	.07	− .88	.43
C_4	− .33	.00	.35	.87

EXHIBIT A-3

Initial and Terminal Factor Patterns;
Attitude Survey Motivation Items;
Hourly Maintenance Workers; $N = 79$

	Initial Pattern				Terminal Pattern				Communality
	C_1	C_2	C_3	C_4	T_1	T_2	T_3	T_4	
Events or Conditions									
Promotion	.45	− .19	.21	.11	.33	.25	.35	− .03	.29
Permissive supervision	.82	.13	− .18	− .03	.81	.08	.06	.24	.72
Interesting work	.86	.16	− .19	− .14	.83	.07	.05	.36	.83
Supervision of others	.62	− .32	− .20	.21	.58	.48	.02	− .07	.57
Raise	.62	.14	.40	.10	.52	− .06	.55	.03	.58
Successful completion of a task	.84	.27	− .17	− .06	.85	− .05	.06	.28	.81
Praise	.71	.26	.01	.05	.71	− .09	.19	.13	.57
Increased status	.40	− .30	− .17	− .21	.28	.40	− .02	.29	.32
Work of subordinates	.64	− .25	− .21	.13	.60	.41	.01	.02	.53
Feelings									
Accomplishment	.89	.19	− .08	.07	.89	.03	.17	.16	.85
Confidence	.90	.26	− .17	− .10	.89	− .02	.08	.34	.91
Recognition	.85	.02	− .13	.10	.83	.19	.12	.11	.75
Pride	.87	.11	− .17	.08	.87	.11	.08	.14	.80
Security	.70	.09	.05	.08	.66	.06	.24	.08	.50
Financial progress	.78	− .19	.25	− .27	.53	.31	.48	.42	.78
Personal growth	.75	− .04	.13	.07	.65	.18	.34	.10	.58
Responsibility	.69	− .33	− .05	− .05	.54	.48	.18	.19	.59
Importance	.56	.08	.39	− .25	.36	− .02	.53	.35	.53
Acceptance	.78	.06	.09	.05	.71	.10	.31	.13	.63
Percentage contribution to variance					72	09	12	07	

Transformation Matrix

	T_1	T_2	T_3	T_4
C_1	.90	.22	.29	.23
C_2	.24	− .96	− .09	.06
C_3	− .25	− .16	.95	− .07
C_4	.25	.00	.00	− .97

EXHIBIT A-4

Initial and Terminal Factor Patterns;
Attitude Survey Motivation Items;
Salaried Supervisors and Managers; $N = 44$

	Initial Pattern				Terminal Pattern				Communality
	C_1	C_2	C_3	C_4	T_1	T_2	T_3	T_4	
Events or Conditions									
Promotion	.57	− .25	− .50	− .12	.55	.28	.37	− .39	.65
Permissive supervision	.70	.51	.25	.27	.50	.45	− .05	.67	.89
Interesting work	.87	.16	− .03	− .17	.80	.42	− .05	.09	.83
Supervision of others	.84	.08	− .19	.10	.71	.43	.26	.13	.76
Raise	.64	− .19	− .36	.16	.56	.24	.48	− .08	.60
Successful completion	.70	.51	.25	.27	.50	.45	− .05	.67	.89
of a task	.73	.33	.15	.06	.60	.39	− .07	.40	.67
Praise	.78	− .10	.27	.25	.74	.00	.18	.42	.75
Increased status	.38	− .08	.11	− .14	.42	.01	− .08	.00	.18
Work of subordinates	.72	.34	− .19	− .15	.58	.60	− .04	.06	.69
Feelings									
Accomplishment	.93	.07	− .04	− .19	.88	.38	− .01	.04	.91
Confidence	.86	.16	.24	.17	.75	.24	.05	.47	.85
Recognition	.86	− .08	− .04	− .15	.85	.24	.07	− .01	.77
Pride	.89	− .23	.17	− .18	.95	.02	− .01	.04	.91
Security	.76	− .34	.09	.04	.80	− .08	.22	.06	.70
Financial progress	.75	− .22	− .15	.18	.70	.14	.41	.06	.67
Personal growth	.89	.18	− .10	.13	.74	.46	.20	.25	.85
Responsibility	.84	.26	− .09	− .08	.71	.51	.01	.15	.79
Importance	.48	− .32	.24	.23	.52	− .24	.23	.24	.44
Acceptance	.72	− .11	.13	.27	.66	.05	.27	.33	.62
Percentage contribution to variance					68	15	06	11	

Transformation Matrix

	T_1	T_2	T_3	T_4
C_1	.93	.31	.14	.17
C_2	− .27	.76	− .40	.43
C_3	.15	− .56	− .55	.60
C_4	− .20	− .07	.72	.66

Appendix B

The Hackman Job Satisfaction Schedule[*]

Name _____ Date _____

All of us have had and will continue to have the experience of being made either very happy or very unhappy about things that happen at work. Some of these experiences are of short duration; some last for longer periods of time. Some occur suddenly in response to a particular thing that happens, and some build up over a period of time. Most of them are violent enough so that we remember later on what happened and how we felt at the time.

We would like you to think of times during the past few years when you got a *real kick* out of your job or were *very happy* on the job. Look at the list below of things that could have happened. Check in the left-hand column the thing or things that you remember as being the primary cause of your being made happy. In the right-hand column check those things that you remember as being of somewhat less significance. Leave blank anything you remember as being of little or no significance to you.

☐ ☐ 1. You were promoted?
☐ ☐ 2. You were allowed to do a piece of work your own way?
☐ ☐ 3. Your work was interesting and challenging to you?
☐ ☐ 4. You were asked to supervise or oversee the work of others?

[*] By Ray C. Hackman, Psychological Service of Pittsburgh.

☐ ☐   5. You got a raise in pay?
☐ ☐   6. You completed a piece of work to your own satisfaction?
☐ ☐   7. You were praised for the way you handled a piece of work?
☐ ☐   8. Your relative position or standing was made apparent to others?

☐ ☐   9. Your subordinates turned out a particularly fine piece of work?

☐ ☐ 10. Other (please specify) _____

The next set of items describes feelings that you might have had at the time. Those that were the strongest and the most vivid should be checked in the left-hand column. The weaker or less characteristic ones should be checked in the right-hand column. Do not check either box before an item if you didn't experience the particular feeling at all. Did what happened make you feel:

☐ ☐   1. That you had really accomplished something?
☐ ☐   2. Confident?
☐ ☐   3. That you and your work were being recognized?
☐ ☐   4. Proud?
☐ ☐   5. Secure?
☐ ☐   6. That you were making material and financial progress?
☐ ☐   7. That you were growing and developing as a person?
☐ ☐   8. Responsible for others and the company?
☐ ☐   9. Important?
☐ ☐ 10. That you belonged or were accepted by the people you worked with?

☐ ☐ 11. Other (please specify) _____

Now, think about times during the past few years when you were very *unhappy* on your job. Look at the list below of things that might have produced this unhappiness. Check in the left-hand column the thing or things you remember as being the primary cause of your unhappiness. In the right-hand column check those things that you remember as being of somewhat less significance. Leave blank any item that was of little or no significance to you.

☐ ☐   1. You didn't get an expected promotion or were demoted?

☐ ☐ 2. You had to do your work exactly the way you were told to?

☐ ☐ 3. Your work was dull and uninteresting?

☐ ☐ 4. You didn't get an expected raise or had your pay cut?

☐ ☐ 5. You were unable to complete an assigned task?

☐ ☐ 6. Your work wasn't noticed or praised when you thought it should have been?

☐ ☐ 7. You couldn't agree with the company's goals?

☐ ☐ 8. Your supervisor criticized your work no matter what you did or how you did it?

☐ ☐ 9. Your supervisor was unfriendly?

☐ ☐ 10. Your supervisor was incompetent?

☐ ☐ 11. You weren't getting along with your subordinates or the people you were working with?

☐ ☐ 12. You couldn't do your job because of the way in which your work was organized?

☐ ☐ 13. Something happened that made you lose face?

☐ ☐ 14. You didn't like the company's personnel policies or procedures?

☐ ☐ 15. Your subordinates turned out a poor piece of work?

☐ ☐ 16. Other (please specify) ⸻⸻⸻⸻⸻

The next set of items describes feelings that you might have had at the time. Those that were the strongest and the most vivid should be checked in the left-hand column. The weaker or less characteristic ones should be checked in the right-hand column. Do not check either box before an item if you didn't experience the particular feeling at all. Did what happen make you feel:

☐ ☐ 1. Blocked from growing or developing?

☐ ☐ 2. That you were not accomplishing anything?

☐ ☐ 3. That you were not being recognized?

☐ ☐ 4. That you were not making financial progress?

☐ ☐ 5. That things were unfair?

☐ ☐ 6. Just plain mad?

☐ ☐ 7. Disgusted?

☐ ☐ 8. Unimportant?

☐ ☐ 9. Insecure?

☐ ☐ 10. Inadequate?
☐ ☐ 11. Less confident?
☐ ☐ 12. Isolated?
☐ ☐ 13. Ashamed of yourself?
☐ ☐ 14. Rejected?
☐ ☐ 15. Anxious or fearful?
☐ ☐ 16. Other (please specify)_____

Statistically Significant Items on Each Guilford-Zimmerman Temperament
Survey Scale for Each High-Low HJSS Factor Comparison,
Together with the Response More Characteristic
of the High Group than the Low Group

Item Number	High A vs Low A		High B vs Low B				High C vs Low C		High N vs Low N		
	A_1	A_2	B_1	B_2	B_3	B_4	C_1	C_2	N_1	N_2	N_3
			G (General Activity)								
1											
6							N*				
11			Y*								
16	Y*										
21			N*						Y†		
26	Y*										
31			N†								
36											
41											
46			Y*								
51			Y*							N*	

* Significant at the .05 level.
†Significant at the .01 level.
‡Significant at the .001 level.

Item Number	High A vs Low A		High B vs Low B				High C vs Low C		High N vs Low N		
	A_1	A_2	B_1	B_2	B_3	B_4	C_1	C_2	N_1	N_2	N_3
56			Y‡						N*		
61									Y†		
66									Y†		
71			Y*								
76											
81			N*						Y*		
86											
91			N*						Y*		
96			Y‡								
101			Y*								
106			N*								
111			Y†								
116	N*										
121			Y*								
126								Y*			
131			Y†								
136											
141								Y‡			
146											
Totals	3	0	15	0	0	0	0	3	7	0	0

<u>R (Restraint)</u>

Item Number	A_1	A_2	B_1	B_2	B_3	B_4	C_1	C_2	N_1	N_2	N_3
2						Y†					
7											
12							N*				
17							Y*				
22											
27											
32							Y*				
37											
42	Y‡										
47						N*					
52									Y†		
57											
62						Y†					
67											
72						N*					
77					N*			Y‡		N*	
82	Y*										
87										Y‡	
92		Y*									
97											
102							Y†				

Item Number	High A vs Low A		High B vs Low B				High C vs Low C		High N vs Low N		
	A_1	A_2	B_1	B_2	B_3	B_4	C_1	C_2	N_1	N_2	N_3
107											
112						Y*					
117						N*					
122	Y*										
127						N†					
132										N*	
137										N†	
142											
147											
Totals	3	1	0	0	1	7	4	1	1	4	0

<u>A (Ascendance)</u>

Item Number	A_1	A_2	B_1	B_2	B_3	B_4	C_1	C_2	N_1	N_2	N_3
3											
8										Y*	
13											
18											
23											
28				N‡							
33				N*				N*			
38				Y†							
43				N*							
48				N‡							
53				Y*							
58											
63											
68		Y*									
73				Y*							
78								Y*			
83				N*							
88											
93											
98								Y*			
103										Y*	
108				N†							
113											
118											
123		Y*									
128						Y†					
133											
138				Y†							
143				N*							
148		Y†									
Totals	0	3	0	11	0	1	0	3	0	2	0

Item Number	High A vs Low A		High B vs Low B				High C vs Low C		High N vs Low N		
	A_1	A_2	B_1	B_2	B_3	B_4	C_1	C_2	N_1	N_2	N_3
					S (Sociability)						
4											
9											
14											
19											
24							Y°				
29											
34					N‡					Y†	
39							Y°				
44											
49											
54											
59							Y°				
64											
69				N°							
74											
79					Y°		Y°				
84											
89							N†				
94											
99	Y†										
104				Y°							
109											
114						N‡					
119							Y°				
124											
129											
134	N†										
139											
144											
149											
Totals	2	0	0	2	1	2	6	0	0	1	0
				E (Emotional Stability)							
5											
10	Y†								Y°		
15										Y°	
20						Y°				N°	
25										Y†	
30	N°										
35											
40											

Item Number	High A vs Low A		High B vs Low B				High C vs Low C		High N vs Low N		
	A_1	A_2	B_1	B_2	B_3	B_4	C_1	C_2	N_1	N_2	N_3
45											
50										Y†	
55										Y°	
60										Y‡	
65									N°		
70											
75											
80						N°					
85											
90											
95										Y†	
100						N°					
105											
110										N‡	
115						Y°				N°	
120											
125											
130						N°				Y°	
135											
140											
145									Y°		
150										N†	
Totals	2	0	0	0	0	5	0	0	3	11	0

$$O \text{ (Objectivity)}$$

Item Number	A_1	A_2	B_1	B_2	B_3	B_4	C_1	C_2	N_1	N_2	N_3
151				Y°							N‡
156											
161											
166											
171				N°							
176		Y°									Y°
181											
186											
191											
196		N°								N°	
201											
206											
211						N°		Y°			Y°
216											
221											Y°
226							Y°				
231		N°									
236										Y†	

Item Number	High A vs Low A		High B vs Low B				High C vs Low C		High N vs Low N		
	A_1	A_2	B_1	B_2	B_3	B_4	C_1	C_2	N_1	N_2	N_3
241											Y‡
246											Y†
251										N‡	
256											
261										Y‡	
266		Y*					Y*				
271											
276											Y†
281					N*						
286							Y*				
291					N*						
296											
Totals	0	4	0	0	4	1	3	1	0	4	7

F (Friendliness)

Item Number	A_1	A_2	B_1	B_2	B_3	B_4	C_1	C_2	N_1	N_2	N_3
152											Y*
157											
162								Y*			
167					N*						
172											
177											Y‡
182				N†							
187		Y*			N*						
192							N*				Y*
197											
202		Y*			N*						Y*
207											Y*
212											
217								Y*			
222											
227											
232											
237											
242		Y*									
247											Y‡
252								Y*			
257											Y*
262	Y*										
267					N*						Y†
272				Y*							
277											
282											
287											
292							N*				Y‡
297								Y*			
Totals	1	3	0	2	4	0	2	4	0	0	9

Item Number	High A vs Low A		High B vs Low B				High C vs Low C		High N vs Low N		
	A_1	A_2	B_1	B_2	B_3	B_4	C_1	C_2	N_1	N_2	N_3
					T (Thoughtfulness)						
153							N*				
158		Y*									
163											
168											
173											
178											
183						Y*				Y*	
188											
193											
198											
203											
208										Y†	
213											
218		Y†								Y*	
223											
228						Y*					
233											
238		Y*									
243										Y‡	
248										Y*	
253						N*				Y†	
258		Y†									
263											
268										Y*	
273		Y*									
		Y*								Y*	
283							N†				
288											
293		Y*									
298											
Totals	0	7	0	0	0	3	2	0	0	8	0
					P (Personal Relations)						
154											
159					Y†						
164											
169											
174											
179											
184											
189											Y*
194					N*						Y*
199											N*
204											Y*
209											

Item Number	High A vs Low A		High B vs Low B				High C vs Low C		High N vs Low N		
	A_1	A_2	B_1	B_2	B_3	B_4	C_1	C_2	N_1	N_2	N_3
214											
219		N*									
224											
229											
234					Y‡						
239											
244					N*						
249											
254											
259											Y*
264					Y*						
269											
274					N†						
279					Y‡						N*
284											Y‡
289											
294											
299											
Totals	0	1	0	0	7	0	0	0	0	0	7

Appendix D

EXHIBIT D-1

Initial and Terminal Factor Patterns;
17- and 18-year-old Women College Students;
Sample A; N = 116

Motivation Scale	Initial Pattern				Terminal Pattern				Communality
	C_1	C_2	C_3	C_4	T_1	T_2	T_3	T_4	
B_1	.59	− .34	.29	− .24	− .07	.34	.65	.25	.61
B_2	.38	− .38	− .19	− .13	− .15	.35	.14	.42	.34
B_3	.33	.34	− .36	− .13	− .58	− .11	− .03	.10	.36
B_4	.40	.22	− .19	− .18	− .48	− .04	.16	.12	.27
C_1	.49	− .22	− .20	.30	− .31	.57	.01	.06	.42
C_2	.34	− .55	.31	.13	.21	.58	.37	.09	.53
A_1	.28	− .61	− .16	.06	.05	.57	.04	.40	.49
A_2	− .20	− .56	− .20	− .27	.33	.10	− .12	.57	.46
N_1	− .71	− .09	− .39	.19	.33	− .16	− .75	.06	.70
N_2	− .55	− .45	− .27	− .13	.47	− .05	− .43	.42	.58
N_3	− .47	− .50	.26	− .16	.70	− .02	.00	.22	.54
Contribution to variance					1.67	1.28	1.37	.99	5.30
Percentage contribution					31	24	26	19	

Transformation Matrix

	T_1	T_2	T_3	T_4
C_1	− .67	.49	.56	.08
C_2	− .52	− .63	− .03	− .55
C_3	.50	− .05	.71	− .49
C_4	.00	.61	− .43	− .67

EXHIBIT D-2

Initial and Terminal Factor Patterns;
17- and 18-Year-Old Women Mushroom-Picker Applicants;
Sample B; $N = 114$

Motivation Scale	Initial Pattern				Terminal Pattern				Communality
	C_1	C_2	C_3	C_4	T_1	T_2	T_3	T_4	
B_1	.46	.48	− .09	.20	− .02	.70	− .02	− .02	.49
B_2	.46	.49	− .08	− .28	− .13	.58	− .03	.43	.54
B_3	.67	− .11	.39	− .10	− .51	.25	− .54	.06	.62
B_4	.48	.10	− .19	− .23	− .38	.34	.07	.25	.33
C_1	.57	.24	.29	− .04	− .23	.47	− .42	.12	.47
C_2	.23	.63	.05	.17	.26	.63	− .10	.06	.48
A_1	− .21	.59	.28	.25	.62	.31	− .22	− .03	.53
A_2	− .48	.58	.13	− .26	.67	.03	− .01	.45	.65
N_1	− .73	− .03	.07	− .15	.50	− .52	.11	.13	.56
N_2	− .79	.22	.24	− .10	.74	− .40	− .04	.17	.74
N_3	− .70	.46	− .15	.09	.79	− .06	.31	.08	.73
Contribution to variance					2.80	2.15	.64	.52	6.14
Percentage contribution					46	35	10	09	

Transformation Matrix

	T_1	T_2	T_3	T_4
C_1	− .74	.62	− .24	.00
C_2	.60	.72	.00	.35
C_3	.18	− .16	− .97	.00
C_4	.23	.26	.00	− .94

EXHIBIT D-3

**Initial and Terminal Factor Patterns;
Women Bank Tellers;
Sample C; N = 37**

Motivation Scale	Initial Pattern				Terminal Pattern				Communality
	C_1	C_2	C_3	C_4	T_1	T_2	T_3	T_4	
B_1	.38	− .53	.35	.18	− .11	.75	− .07	.04	.58
B_2	.65	− .31	− .23	− .15	− .46	.37	.49	.04	.59
B_3	.63	.27	.16	− .18	− .57	.09	.07	− .43	.53
B_4	.65	− .14	− .14	.27	− .61	.33	.09	.21	.54
C_1	.62	− .22	− .22	− .18	− .45	.29	.47	− .01	.51
C_2	.31	− .56	− .11	− .22	− .03	.48	.48	.07	.47
A_1	− .18	− .60	.11	− .32	.48	.41	.32	− .03	.51
A_2	− .41	− .40	− .25	.11	.43	.05	.12	.45	.40
N_1	− .80	.27	− .24	− .19	.60	− .61	.00	.06	.81
N_2	− .80	− .25	.15	− .16	.86	− .06	− .07	.03	.75
N_3	− .76	− .48	.25	.20	.84	.22	− .28	.29	.91
Contribution to variance					3.34	1.73	.91	.53	6.60
Percentage contribution					51	27	14	08	

Transformation Matrix

	T_1	T_2	T_3	T_4
C_1	− .87	.39	.22	− .17
C_2	− .37	− .78	− .35	− .37
C_3	.19	.47	− .60	− .62
C_4	− .25	.11	− .69	.67

EXHIBIT D-4

Initial and Terminal Factor Patterns;
Production Management Trainee Applicants;
Sample D; $N = 188$

Motivation Scale	Initial Pattern				Terminal Pattern				Communality
	C_1	C_2	C_3	C_4	T_1	T_2	T_3	T_4	
B_1	.33	.50	− .31	.42	.57	− .14	.54	.06	.64
B_2	.36	.46	.27	− .45	.28	.46	.03	− .57	.62
B_3	.67	− .28	− .25	− .14	.07	− .52	.05	− .57	.60
B_4	.59	.23	.21	.10	.57	− .06	− .05	− .35	.45
C_1	.39	.39	− .31	− .29	.15	.07	.48	− .48	.49
C_2	− .18	.56	− .24	− .18	.00	.42	.51	.00	.44
A_1	− .19	.53	− .37	− .08	− .01	.30	.60	.08	.46
A_2	− .48	.25	.17	.17	.01	.37	.00	.46	.35
N_1	− .66	− .40	− .16	− .30	− .79	.09	− .09	.25	.70
N_2	− .74	− .11	− .05	.15	− .40	.16	− .02	.63	.58
N_3	− .68	.37	.07	− .04	− .19	.59	.15	.45	.61
Contribution to variance					1.58	1.30	1.18	1.89	5.94
Percentage contribution					27	22	20	31	

Transformation Matrix

	T_1	T_2	T_3	T_4
C_1	.56	− .44	.00	− .71
C_2	.51	.65	.56	.00
C_3	.34	.44	− .83	.00
C_4	.56	− .44	.00	.71

EXHIBIT D-5

Initial and Terminal Factor Patterns;
Sales Management Trainee Applicants;
Sample E; $N = 109$

Motivation Scale	Initial Pattern				Terminal Pattern				
	C_1	C_2	C_3	C_4	T_1	T_2	T_3	T_4	Communality
B_1	.24	− .55	− .09	.34	.03	.69	.11	.06	.48
B_2	.31	− .24	.32	− .33	− .27	.05	.06	.53	.36
B_3	.63	.11	.16	.11	− .64	.19	.00	.00	.45
B_4	.63	− .30	− .23	− .25	− .34	.42	− .43	.36	.61
C_1	.40	.18	.39	.11	− .55	− .02	.24	.01	.36
C_2	− .25	− .23	.56	.08	.12	− .06	.60	.24	.44
A_1	− .43	− .21	.49	.30	.28	− .02	.69	.01	.56
A_2	− .58	− .29	− .23	− .06	.69	.00	− .02	.04	.48
N_1	− .63	.49	.06	− .27	.34	− .76	.01	− .14	.71
N_2	− .73	− .14	− .30	.21	.78	− .02	.06	− .29	.70
N_3	− .63	− .41	− .07	− .26	.73	− .08	.05	.31	.64
Contribution to variance					2.73	1.27	1.10	.67	5.79
Percentage contribution					47	22	19	12	

Transformation Matrix

	T_1	T_2	T_3	T_4
C_1	− .86	.42	− .26	.14
C_2	− .39	− .72	− .15	− .56
C_3	− .33	− .28	.83	.36
C_4	− .03	.49	.47	− .73

EXHIBIT D-6

Initial and Terminal Factor Patterns;
Industrial Payroll Employees;
Sample F; $N = 102$

Motivation Scale	Initial Pattern				Terminal Pattern				Communality
	C_1	C_2	C_3	C_4	T_1	T_2	T_3	T_4	
B_1	.54	− .20	.30	− .18	− .14	.65	.11	.08	.45
B_2	.57	− .32	− .18	− .22	− .38	.38	.23	.42	.51
B_3	.50	.26	− .44	− .13	− .72	− .01	.02	.08	.53
B_4	.36	− .05	− .31	− .21	− .42	.09	.05	.29	.27
C_1	.57	− .17	− .26	.32	− .41	.12	.58	.06	.52
C_2	.41	− .56	.34	.19	.19	.56	.52	.12	.63
A_1	.19	− .75	.16	.13	.32	.37	.52	.37	.65
A_2	− .24	− .56	− .23	− .22	.26	− .11	.06	.62	.47
N_1	− .67	− .28	− .19	.18	.51	− .54	.07	.20	.60
N_2	− .69	− .37	− .13	.15	.60	− .48	.07	.25	.66
N_3	− .51	− .61	.11	− .21	.66	− .04	− .06	.50	.69
Contribution to variance					2.29	1.57	.96	1.16	5.98
Percentage contribution					38	26	16	.20	

Transformation Matrix

	T_1	T_2	T_3	T_4
C_1	− .69	.63	.36	− .02
C_2	− .46	− .24	− .50	− .70
C_3	.54	.68	− .17	− .47
C_4	.15	− .31	.77	− .54

EXHIBIT D-7

Initial and Terminal Factor Patterns;
Hourly Industrial Workers;
Sample G; $N = 120$

Motivation Scale	Initial Pattern				Terminal Pattern				Communality
	C_1	C_2	C_3	C_4	T_1	T_2	T_3	T_4	
B_1	.35	− .38	− .33	.28	− .06	.35	− .01	.58	.46
B_2	.52	− .47	.15	− .22	− .47	.42	.37	.14	.56
B_3	.67	.16	.19	− .28	− .76	− .05	.06	.01	.58
B_4	.70	− .12	− .10	− .24	− .63	.07	.21	.35	.57
C_1	.54	− .36	.12	.14	− .40	.49	.02	.23	.45
C_2	.17	− .69	.18	.09	− .04	.68	.27	.09	.55
A_1	− .13	− .66	.29	.23	.23	.71	.15	− .10	.59
A_2	− .35	− .52	− .05	− .17	.38	.25	.46	− .02	.44
N_1	− .58	− .06	.36	− .22	.36	− .01	.22	− .58	.51
N_2	− .72	− .16	− .10	− .20	.65	− .13	.33	− 22	.60
N_3	− .65	− .44	− .35	.09	.80	.12	.27	.15	.75
Contribution to variance					2.76	1.61	.74	.96	6.06
Percentage contribution					45	27	12	16	

Transformation Matrix

	T_1	T_2	T_3	T_4
C_1	− .89	.18	− .09	.41
C_2	− .20	− .78	− .55	− .23
C_3	− .30	.41	− .12	− .85
C_4	.28	.45	− .82	.23

EXHIBIT D-8

Initial and Terminal Factor Patterns;
Public Utility Operators;
Sample H; $N = 73$

Motivation Scale	Initial Pattern				Terminal Pattern				
	C_1	C_2	C_3	C_4	T_1	T_2	T_3	T_4	Communality
B_1	−.13	.53	−.38	.28	−.02	.11	.69	.18	.52
B_2	.11	.49	.38	−.11	−.11	.62	−.03	.13	.41
B_3	.67	−.17	.21	.14	−.63	.03	−.27	−.28	.55
B_4	.58	.18	−.12	−.26	−.57	.04	−.12	.34	.46
C_1	.29	.37	.29	.08	−.30	.47	.03	−.03	.31
C_2	−.36	.45	.10	.23	.28	.39	.41	−.03	.40
A_1	−.41	.42	.41	.12	.38	.59	.17	−.09	.53
A_2	−.64	.26	.25	−.26	.66	.36	−.01	.21	.61
N_1	−.28	−.57	.48	−.32	.44	−.06	−.71	.21	.73
N_2	−.71	−.34	.08	−.08	.75	−.18	−.12	.12	.62
N_3	−.80	.10	−.10	−.29	.80	.00	.11	.32	.75
Contribution to variance					2.88	1.29	1.28	.45	5.89
Percentage contribution					49	22	22	07	

Transformation Matrix

	T_1	T_2	T_3	T_4
C_1	−.98	.00	−.22	.00
C_2	−.12	.71	.55	.44
C_3	.12	.71	−.55	−.44
C_4	−.13	.00	.60	−.79

EXHIBIT D-9

Initial and Terminal Factor Patterns;
Bank Officers;
Sample I; $N = 42$

Motivation Scale	Initial Pattern				Terminal Pattern				Communality
	C_1	C_2	C_3	C_4	T_1	T_2	T_3	T_4	
B_1	.43	.11	− .47	.41	.00	− .08	.76	− .03	.58
B_2	.63	.45	.24	− .19	.81	− .06	.16	− .11	.70
B_3	.47	− .27	− .23	− .43	.13	− .21	.09	− .68	.53
B_4	.36	− .10	.07	− .11	.22	− .25	.05	− .21	.15
C_1	.55	.21	.40	.05	.63	− .32	.09	.09	.52
C_2	.64	.60	.12	− .06	.81	.05	.35	− .03	.78
A_1	.39	.48	− .19	− .27	.50	.29	.28	− .28	.49
A_2	− .31	.56	− .38	− .13	.01	.74	.15	.02	.57
N_1	− .65	.12	.38	− .52	− .01	.42	− .82	.06	.85
N_2	− .65	.42	− .39	− .24	− .25	.86	− .11	.01	.81
N_3	− .67	.50	.23	.32	− .08	.51	− .20	.75	.85
Contribution to variance					2.09	2.03	1.57	1.15	6.83
Percentage contribution					30	30	23	17	

Transformation Matrix

	T_1	T_2	T_3	T_4
C_1	.60	− .52	.50	− .36
C_2	.60	.69	.23	.32
C_3	.46	− .40	− .64	.46
C_4	− .26	− .30	.53	.75

EXHIBIT D-10

Initial and Terminal Factor Patterns; Research and Development Managers; Sample J; $N = 41$

Motivation Scale	Initial Pattern				Terminal Pattern				Communality
	C_1	C_2	C_3	C_4	T_1	T_2	T_3	T_4	
B_1	− .14	− .56	− .44	.13	− .14	.02	.72	.05	.54
B_2	.16	− .69	.36	.16	.09	.54	.28	.53	.65
B_3	− .59	.28	.21	− .23	− .60	− .07	− .38	− .10	.52
B_4	− .52	− .20	.20	.34	− .47	− .10	.07	.48	.46
C_1	− .33	− .54	.34	− .40	− .48	.65	.09	.08	.67
C_2	.33	− .61	− .31	− .19	.24	.41	.61	− .15	.61
A_1	.23	− .54	− .09	− .22	.13	.46	.41	− .07	.40
A_2	.53	− .24	.27	.18	.50	.30	.02	.32	.45
N_1	.48	.57	.30	− .17	.47	.01	− .64	− .19	.67
N_2	.76	.33	.11	.11	.79	− .04	− .29	− .03	.74
N_3	.68	.20	− .27	.21	.74	− .22	.07	− .11	.61
Contribution to variance					2.60	1.23	1.79	.70	6.32
Percentage contribution					41	20	28	11	

Transformation Matrix

	T_1	T_2	T_3	T_4
C_1	.97	.23	.00	− .09
C_2	.11	− .61	− .72	− .32
C_3	− .07	.49	− .67	.55
C_4	.20	− .58	.18	.77

EXHIBIT D-11

Initial and Terminal Factor Patterns;
Research and Development Managers;
Sample K; $N = 44$

Motivation Scale	Initial Pattern				Terminal Pattern				Communality
	C_1	C_2	C_3	C_4	T_1	T_2	T_3	T_4	
B_1	.59	.04	.24	− .31	− .30	.63	− .03	.13	.50
B_2	.49	− .38	.08	− .07	.04	.42	− .13	.45	.40
B_3	.18	.39	− .54	− .25	− .19	.08	− .57	− .42	.54
B_4	.51	.11	− .11	− .21	− .26	.41	− .31	.03	.33
C_1	.47	− .44	− .26	.37	.05	.00	− .43	.66	.62
C_2	.33	− .69	.21	.17	.26	.24	.05	.73	.66
A_1	.19	− .51	.07	− .33	.38	.47	− .02	.23	.41
A_2	− .26	− .60	− .20	− .21	.71	.07	− .07	.08	.51
N_1	− .73	− .10	− .28	− .17	.57	− .34	.05	− .45	.65
N_2	− .71	− .24	− .34	− .28	.72	− .24	− .01	− .43	.76
N_3	− .55	− .55	.35	− .21	.69	.04	.55	.03	.78
Contribution to variance					2.21	1.21	.94	1.81	6.16
Percentage contribution					36	20	15	29	

Transformation Matrix

	T_1	T_2	T_3	T_4
C_1	− .52	.57	− .42	.48
C_2	− .77	− .18	.00	− .62
C_3	− .24	.26	.91	.22
C_4	− .30	− .76	.00	.59

EXHIBIT D-12

Initial and Terminal Factor Patterns;
Industrial Salesmen;
Sample L; $N = 40$

Motivation Scale	Initial Pattern				Terminal Pattern				Communality
	C_1	C_2	C_3	C_4	T_1	T_2	T_3	T_4	
B_1	.63	− .49	.07	− .31	.76	− .10	.28	− .27	.74
B_2	.48	− .36	− .19	.19	.50	− .08	.32	.27	.43
B_3	.22	.52	.20	.10	− .29	− .52	.07	− .07	.36
B_4	.45	.30	− .31	.36	.07	− .53	.09	.47	.51
C_1	.30	.05	.31	− .26	.13	− .25	.13	− .40	.26
C_2	.58	− .61	.03	.11	.66	.02	.54	.06	.72
A_1	.19	− .66	.34	.24	.29	.33	.67	− .07	.65
A_2	− .14	− .65	.28	.30	.09	.56	.54	.01	.61
N_1	− .79	.17	.25	.23	− .76	.44	− .08	− .01	.76
N_2	− .69	− .21	.16	− .08	− .32	.64	− .13	− .17	.56
N_3	− .52	− .55	− .28	− .20	.20	.76	− .28	.06	.70
Contribution to variance					2.17	2.23	1.33	.57	6.30
Percentage contribution					35	35	21	09	

Transformation Matrix

	T_1	T_2	T_3	T_4
C_1	.60	− .71	.38	.00
C_2	− .60	− .71	− .38	.00
C_3	− .38	.00	.60	− .71
C_4	− .38	.00	.60	.71

EXHIBIT D-13

Initial and Terminal Factor Patterns;
Combined Samples; $N = 921$

Moti-vation Scale	Initial Pattern					Terminal Pattern					Commu-nality
	C_1	C_2	C_3	C_4	C_5	T_1	T_2	T_3	T_4	T_5	
B_1	.40	− .48	.28	.16	.32	.00	.07	.77	− .08	.06	.61
B_2	.41	− .42	− .21	− .07	− .29	− .21	.47	.19	− .05	.42	.48
B_3	.56	.29	− .27	.24	.05	− .52	− .01	.04	− .50	− .01	.52
B_4	.56	− .04	.08	.13	− .33	− .48	.00	.20	− .09	.41	.45
C_1	.48	− .22	− .29	− .13	.03	− .31	.46	.21	− .16	.06	.38
C_2	.10	− .60	− .16	− .27	.16	.18	.58	.34	.11	.01	.50
A_1	− .09	− .59	− .30	− .06	.23	.40	.53	.24	− .10	− .01	.51
A_2	− .44	− .48	− .10	.21	− .17	.61	.13	− .03	− .03	.34	.51
N_1	− .69	.22	− .34	− .13	− .15	.40	.04	− .70	.07	− .13	.67
N_2	− .75	− .15	− .10	.25	.04	.76	− .12	− .26	− .07	.02	.66
N_3	− .63	− .42	.17	− .18	− .11	.65	.10	− .07	.44	.12	.65
Contribution to variance						2.37	1.10	1.45	.52	.50	5.94
Percentage contribution						40	19	24	09	08	

	Transformation Matrix				
	T_1	T_2	T_3	T_4	T_5
C_1	− .82	.18	.48	− .22	.13
C_2	− .48	− .54	− .56	− .10	− .40
C_3	− .02	− .64	.47	.57	.07
C_4	.25	− .52	.16	− .74	.37
C_5	.21	.00	.46	− .24	− .82

EXHIBIT D-14

Terminal Orthogonal (T) and Oblique (V) Factor Patterns; Combined Samples; $N = 921$

Motivation Scale	Orthogonal Pattern					Oblique Pattern				
	T_1	T_2	T_3	T_4	T_5	V_1	V_2	V_3	V_4	V_5
B_1	.00	.07	.77	− .08	.06	− .09	.07	.64	− .08	− .04
B_2	− .21	.47	.19	− .05	.42	− .11	.47	− .02	− .05	.43
B_3	− .52	− .01	.04	− .50	− .01	− .05	− .01	.02	− .50	− .02
B_4	− .48	.00	.20	− .09	.41	− .32	.00	.17	− .09	.39
C_1	− .31	.46	.21	− .16	.06	− .11	.46	− .05	− .16	.07
C_2	.18	.58	.34	.11	.01	.05	.58	.04	.11	.00
A_1	.40	.53	.24	− .10	− .01	.36	.53	.04	− .10	− .01
A_2	.61	.13	− .03	− .03	.34	.48	.13	.07	− .03	.34
N_1	.40	.04	− .70	.07	− .13	.38	.04	− .58	.07	− .04
N_2	.76	− .12	− .26	− .07	.02	.63	− .12	− .03	− .07	.03
N_3	.65	.10	− .07	.44	.12	.20	.10	− .05	.44	.13

	Transformation Matrix						T^1T			
	V_1	V_2	V_3	V_4	V_5		V_1	V_2	V_3	V_4	V_5
T_1	.72	.00	.16	.00	− .02	V_1	1.00	.10	.00	− .66	.00
T_2	.10	1.00	− .46	.00	.07	V_2		1.00	− .46	.00	.07
T_3	− .19	.00	.85	.00	− .13	V_3			1.00	− .14	.00
T_4	− .66	.00	− .14	1.00	.02	V_4				1.00	.02
T_5	.00	.00	.15	.00	.99	V_5					1.00

Appendix E

EXHIBIT E-1

Analysis of Variance — Drive Factor

Source	df	SS	MS	F	p
Criterion groups	1	3,905.73	3,905.73	7.63	<.01
Companies	7	17,312.10	2,473.16	4.83	<.001
Interaction	7	2,836.17	405.17	—	—
Within groups	302	154,502.71	511.60		
Totals	317	178,556.71			

EXHIBIT E-2

Analysis of Variance — Achievement Factor

Source	df	SS	MS	F	p
Criterion groups	1	345.48	345.48	5.54	<.05
Companies	7	4,510.47	644.35	10.33	<.001
Interaction	7	340.40	48.62	—	—
Within groups	302	18,831.03	62.35		
Totals	317	24,027.38			

EXHIBIT E-3

Analysis of Variance — Status Factor

Source	df	SS	MS	F	p
Criterion groups	1	243.01	243.01	5.11	<.05
Companies	7	4,837.06	691.01	14.52	<.001
Interaction	7	409.95	58.56	1.23	>.05
Within groups	302	14,368.28	47.58		
Totals	317	19,858.30			

EXHIBIT E-4

Analysis of Variance — Anxiety Factor

Source	df	SS	MS	F	p
Criterion groups	1	1,474.25	1,474.25	5.42	<.05
Companies	7	14,558.35	2,079.76	7.64	<.001
Interaction	7	3,031.95	433.13	1.59	>.05
Within groups	302	82,183.82	272.13		
Totals	317	101,248.37			

EXHIBIT E-5

Analysis of Variance — Aggression Factor

Source	df	SS	MS	F	p
Criterion groups	1	999.06	999.06	6.71	
Companies	7	4,592.10	656.01	4.41	<.001
Interaction	7	2,057.86	293.98	1.98	<.05
Within groups	302	44,950.44	148.84		
Totals	317	52,599.46			

Bibliography

Barrett, G. V., *Motivation in Industry,* Howard Allen, Cleveland, 1966.

Bendig, A. W., "Age Differences in the Inter-Scale Factor Structure of the Guilford-Zimmerman Temperament Survey," *Journal of Consulting Psychology,* Vol. 24, 1960, pp. 134-138.

Crowne, D. P., and D. Marlowe, *The Approval Motive,* John Wiley, New York, 1964.

Gellerman, S. W., *Motivation and Productivity,* American Management Association, New York, 1963.

Guilford, J. P., *Personality,* McGraw-Hill, New York, 1959.

The Guilford-Zimmerman Temperament Survey, Manual of Instructions and Interpretations, Sheridan Supply Company, Beverly Hills, 1949.

Hackman, R. C., and D. W. Dysinger, *A Theory of Motivation,* Technical Report, The Office of Naval Research, Pittsburgh, Contract Nonr-2810 (00), June 1961.

Harmon, H. H., *Modern Factor Analysis,* The University of Chicago Press, Chicago, 1960.

Heilbroner, R. L., *The Quest for Wealth,* Simon and Schuster, New York, 1956.

Herzberg, F., B. Mausner, R. Peterson, and D. F. Capwell, *Job Attitudes: Review of Research and Opinion,* Psychological Service of Pittsburgh, 1957.

————, B. Mausner, and B. B. Snyderman, *The Motivation to Work,* John Wiley, New York, 1959.

————, *Work and the Nature of Man,* World Publishing, New York, 1966.

Maslow, A. H., "A Theory of Motivation," *Psychological Review,* Vol. 50, 1943, pp. 370 - 396.

McClelland, D. C., J. W. Atkinson, R. A. Clark, and E. L. Lowell, *The Achievement Motive,* Appleton-Century-Crofts, New York, 1953.

————, *The Achieving Society,* D. Van Nostrand, New York, 1961.

McNemar, Q., *Psychological Statistics,* 3rd ed., John Wiley, New York, 1962.

Packard, V., *The Status Seekers,* David McKay, New York, 1959.

Roethlisberger, F. J., and W. J. Dickson, *Management and the Worker,* Harvard University Press, Cambridge, 1933.

Schultz, D. P., *Sensory Restriction: Effects on Behavior,* Academic Press, New York, 1965.

Thurstone, L. L., *Multiple-Factor Analysis,* The University of Chicago Press, Chicago, 1947.

Whyte, W. F., *Money and Motivation,* Harper & Row, New York, 1955.

Whyte, Jr., W. H., *The Organization Man,* Simon and Schuster, New York, 1956.

INDEX

Index

About the Author

Ray C. Hackman is Research Director of Psychological Service of Pittsburgh. He was awarded his A.B. and M.A. from the University of Nebraska, received his Ph.D. from the University of Minnesota, and is a Diplomate in Industrial Psychology. Before assuming his present post in 1958 he was Professor of Psychology at the University of Maryland.

Dr. Hackman is author of many published articles and research reports, and he is a member of the American, Eastern, Pennsylvania, and Pittsburgh Psychological Associations and the Pittsburgh Personnel Association.